Paul Cezanne (France) Inspired Art:

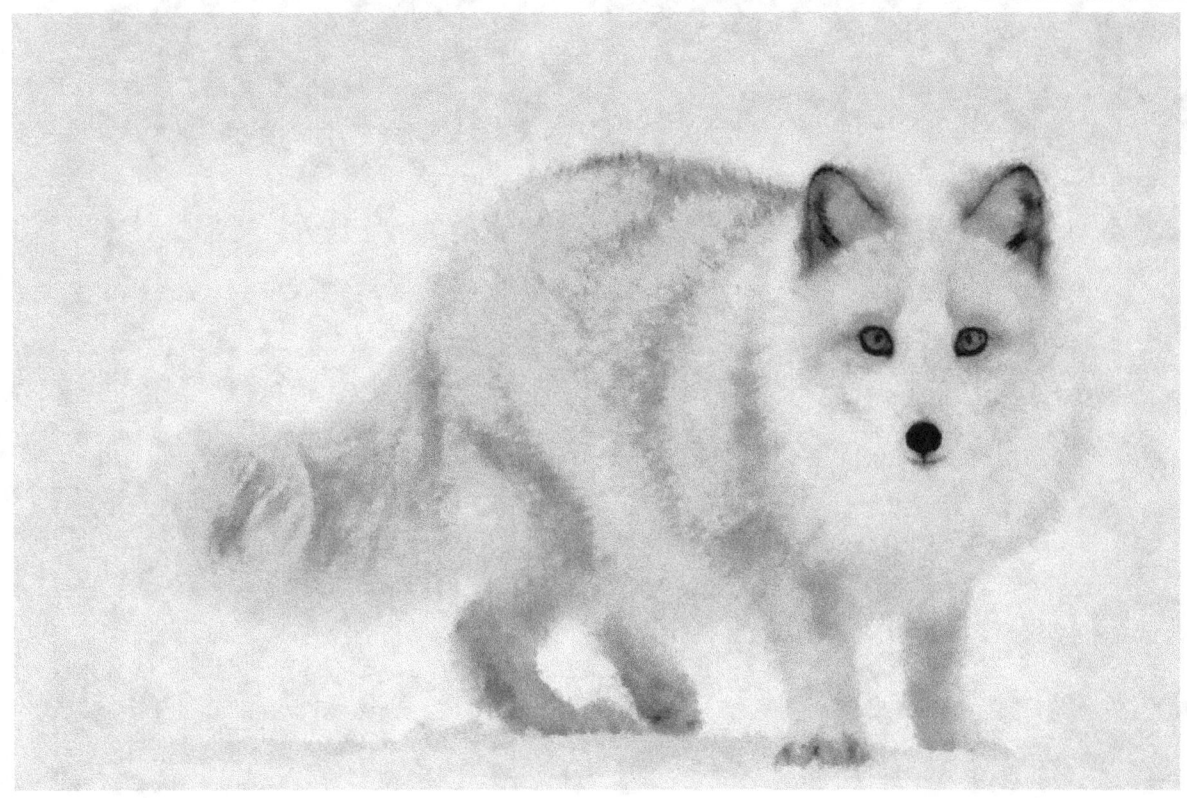

Joaquin Sorolla (Spain):

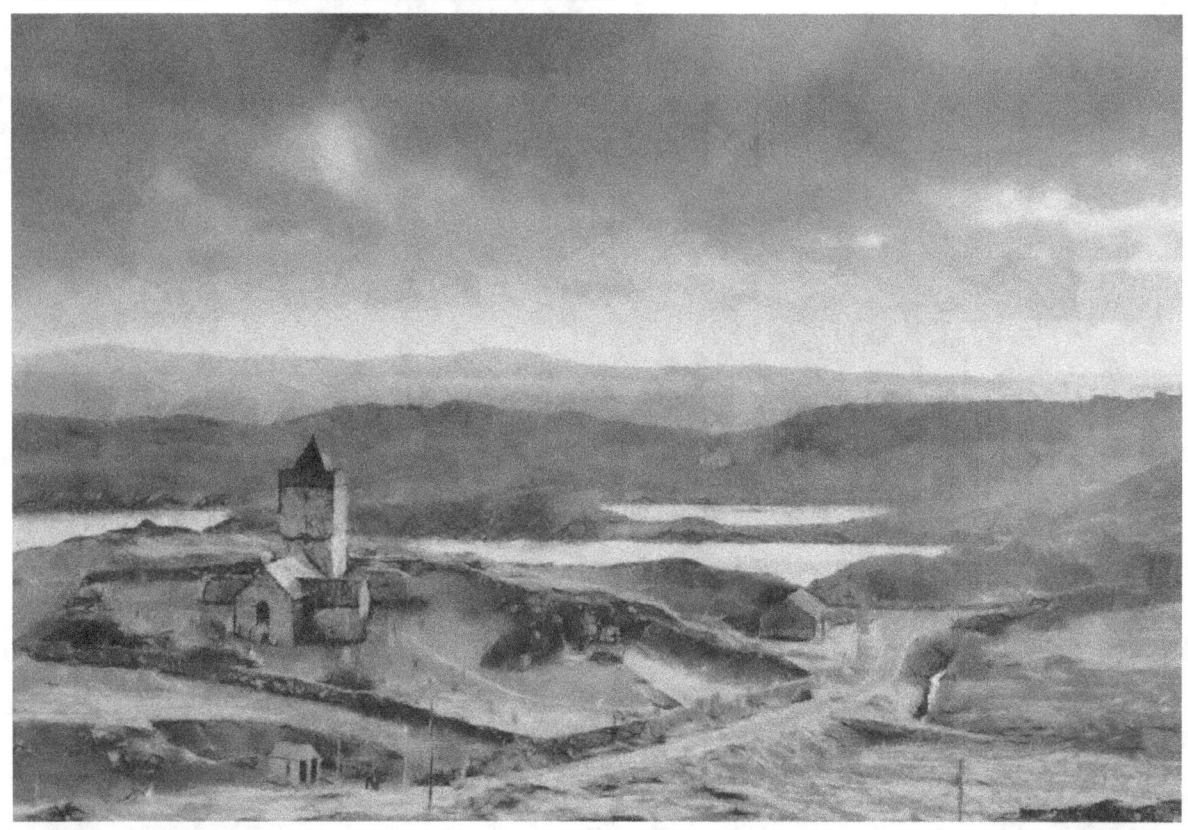

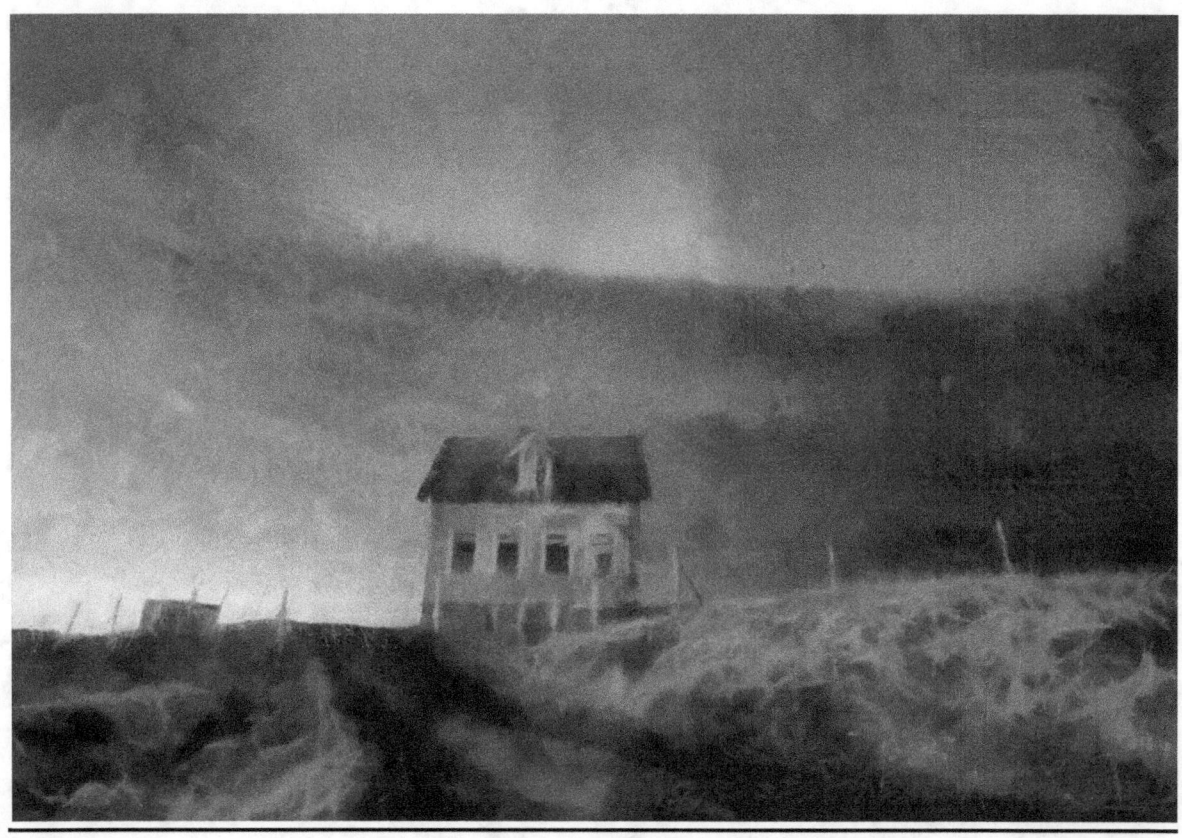

Mona Lisa (Color & Digitally Enhanced)

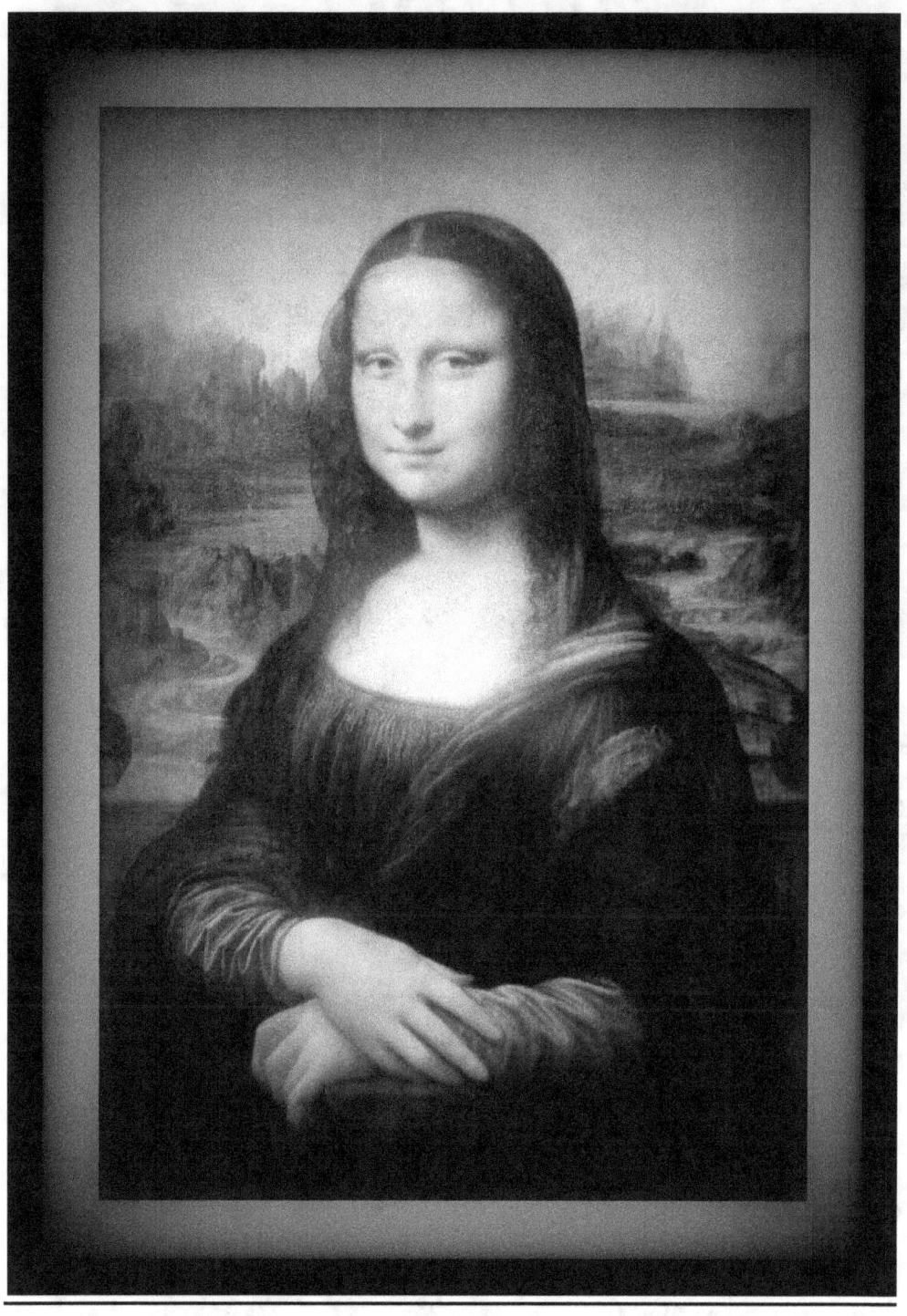

Simulated Chalk Drawing of Some Still Life:
Fruits.

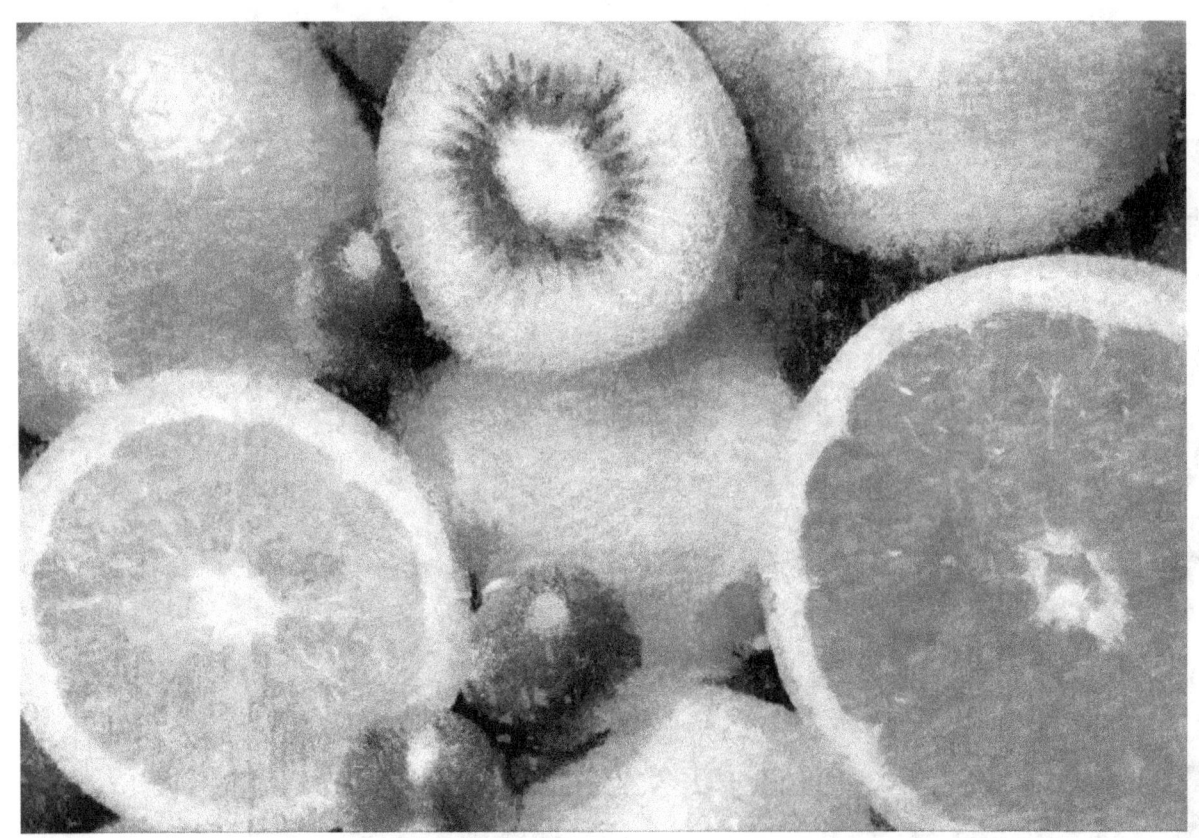

Tree Reflections with Silver & Gold Objects: Modern Art (Silver Pyramid, Gold Base).

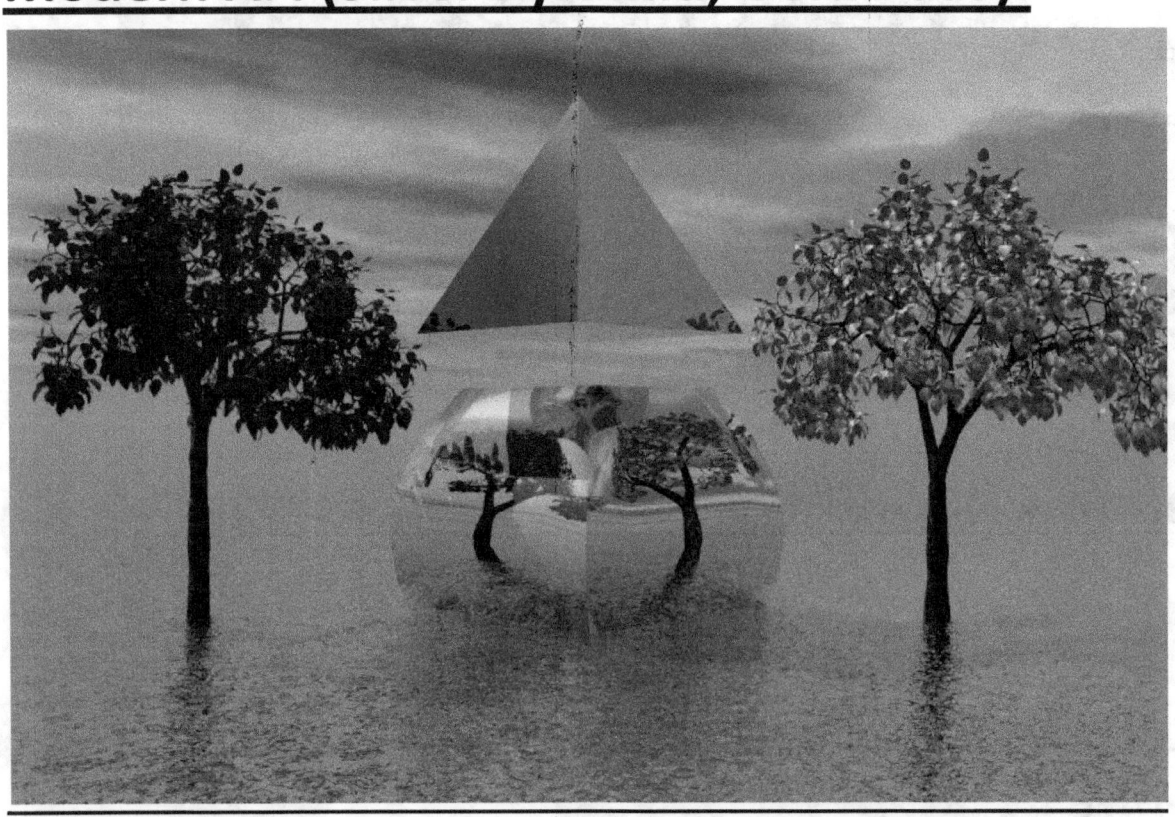

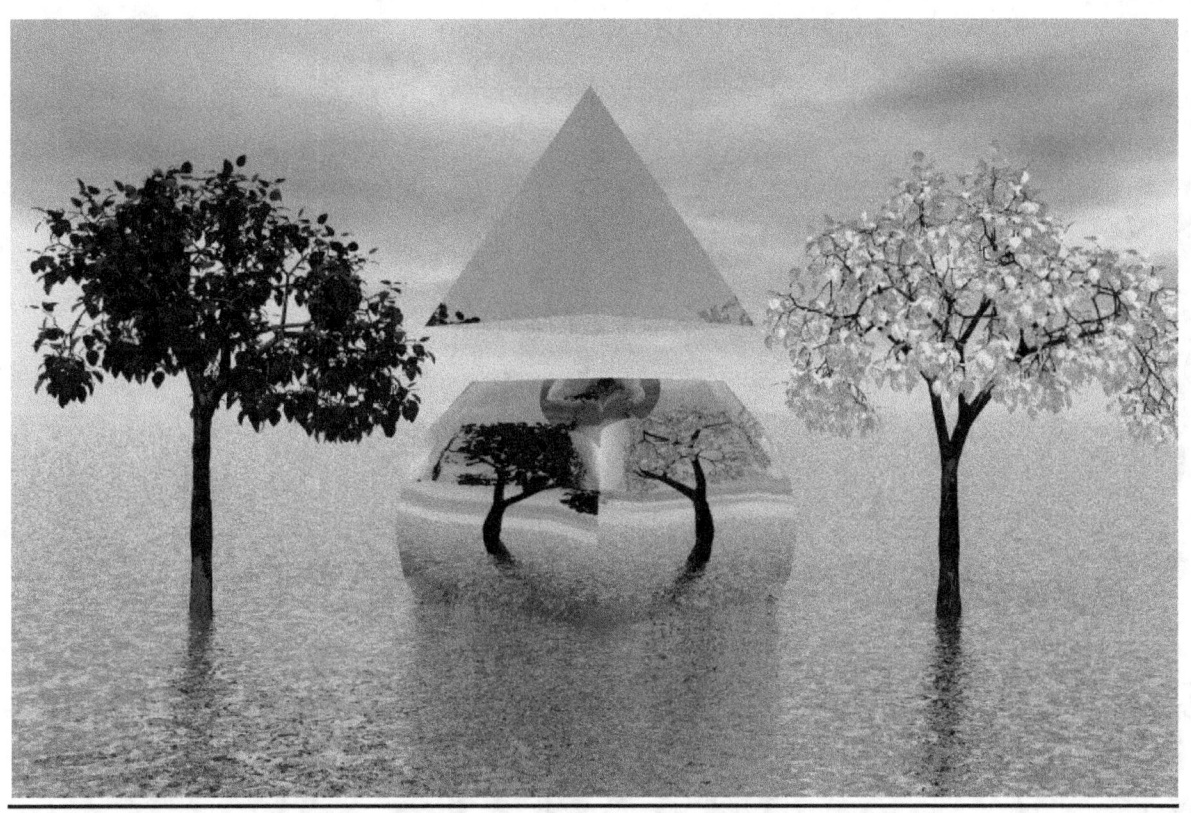

Monet Impressionist Inspired Art:

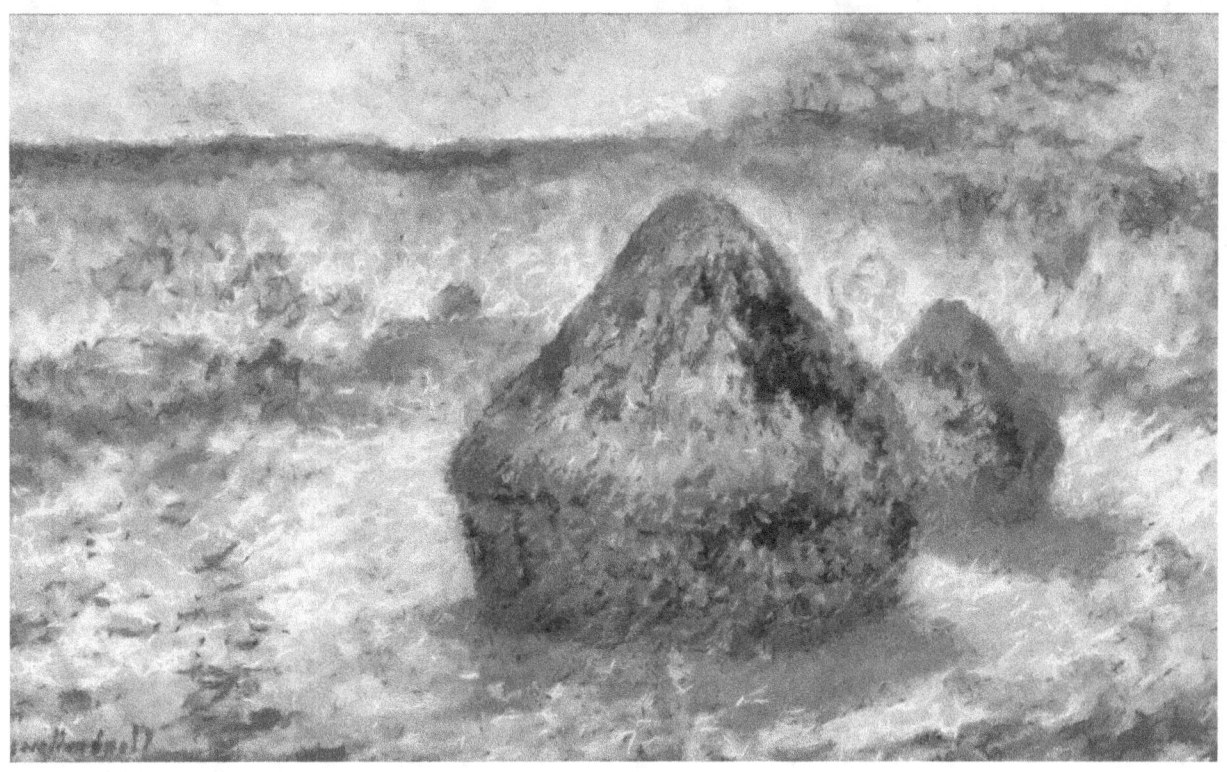

Japanese-Style Art:

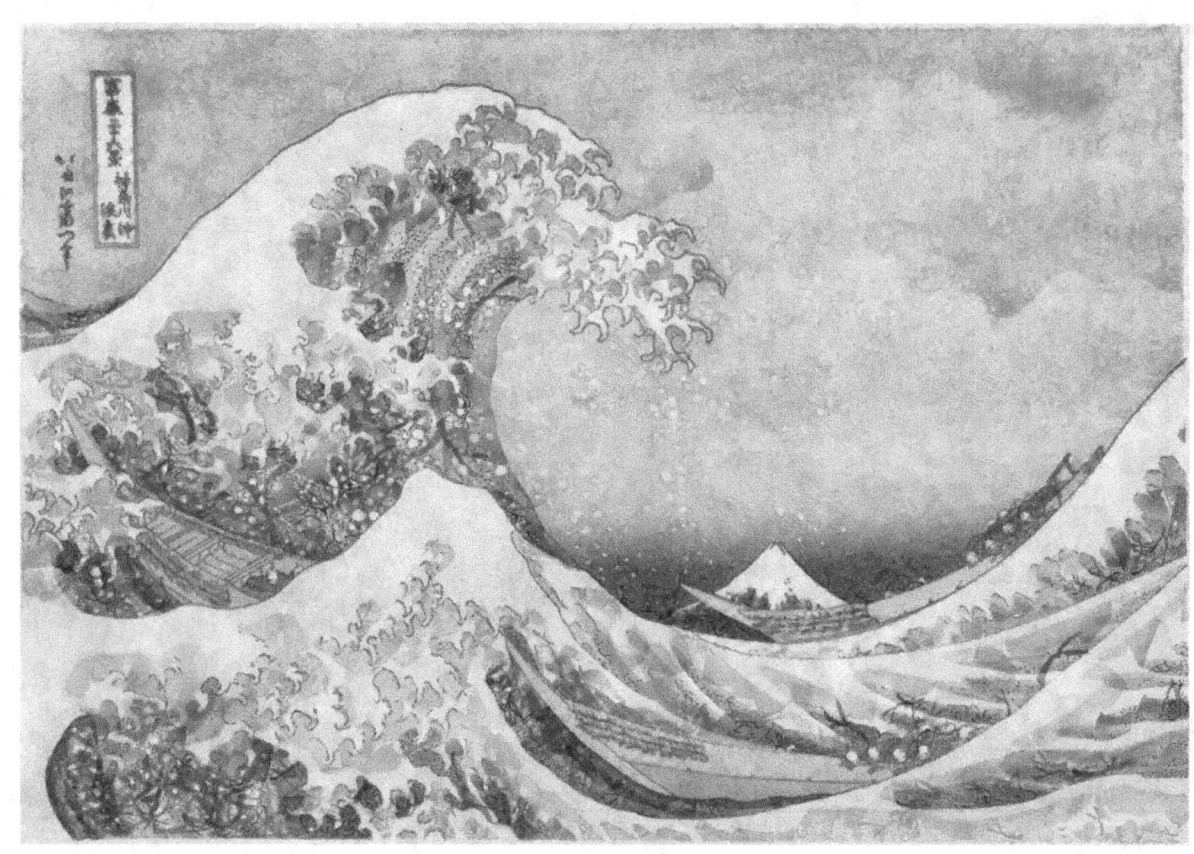

Photo-Realistic Digital Paintwork.

Library of Congress, USA.

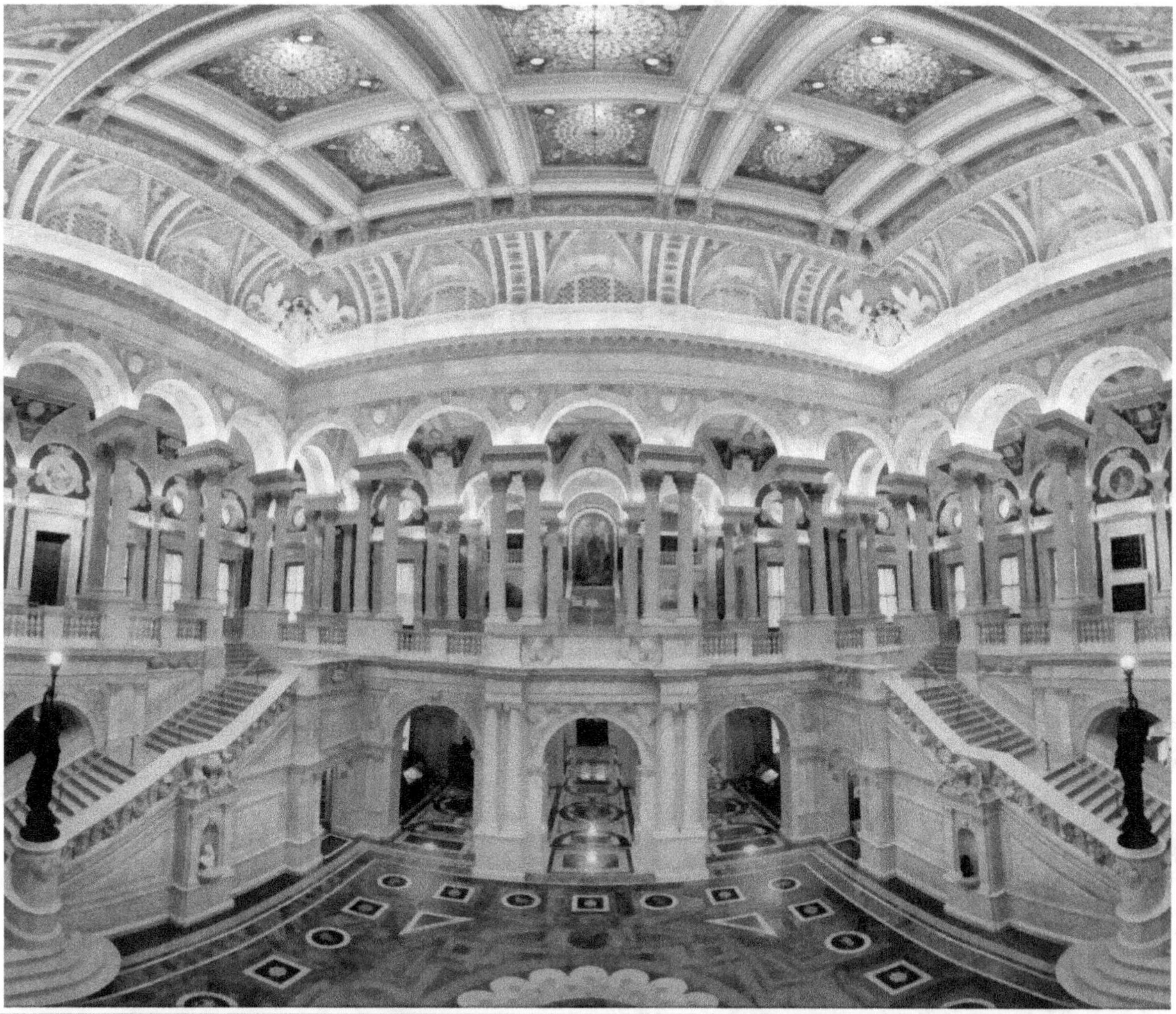

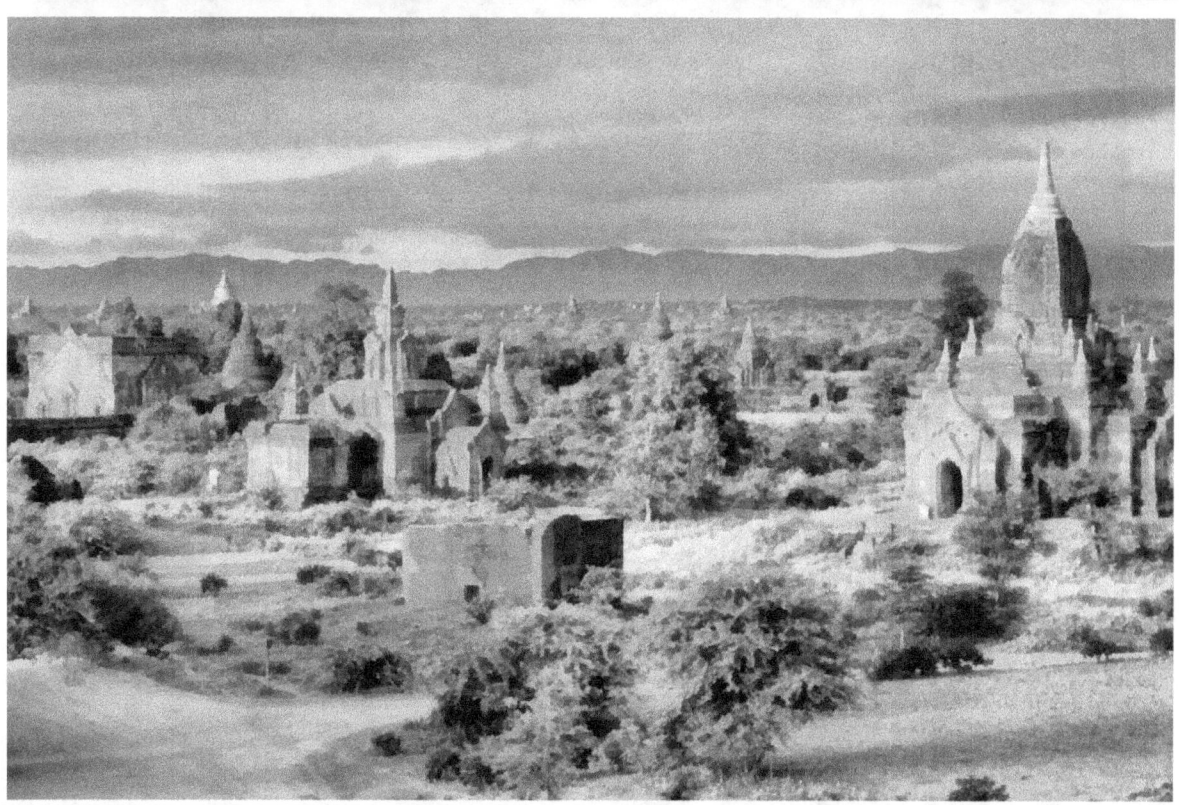

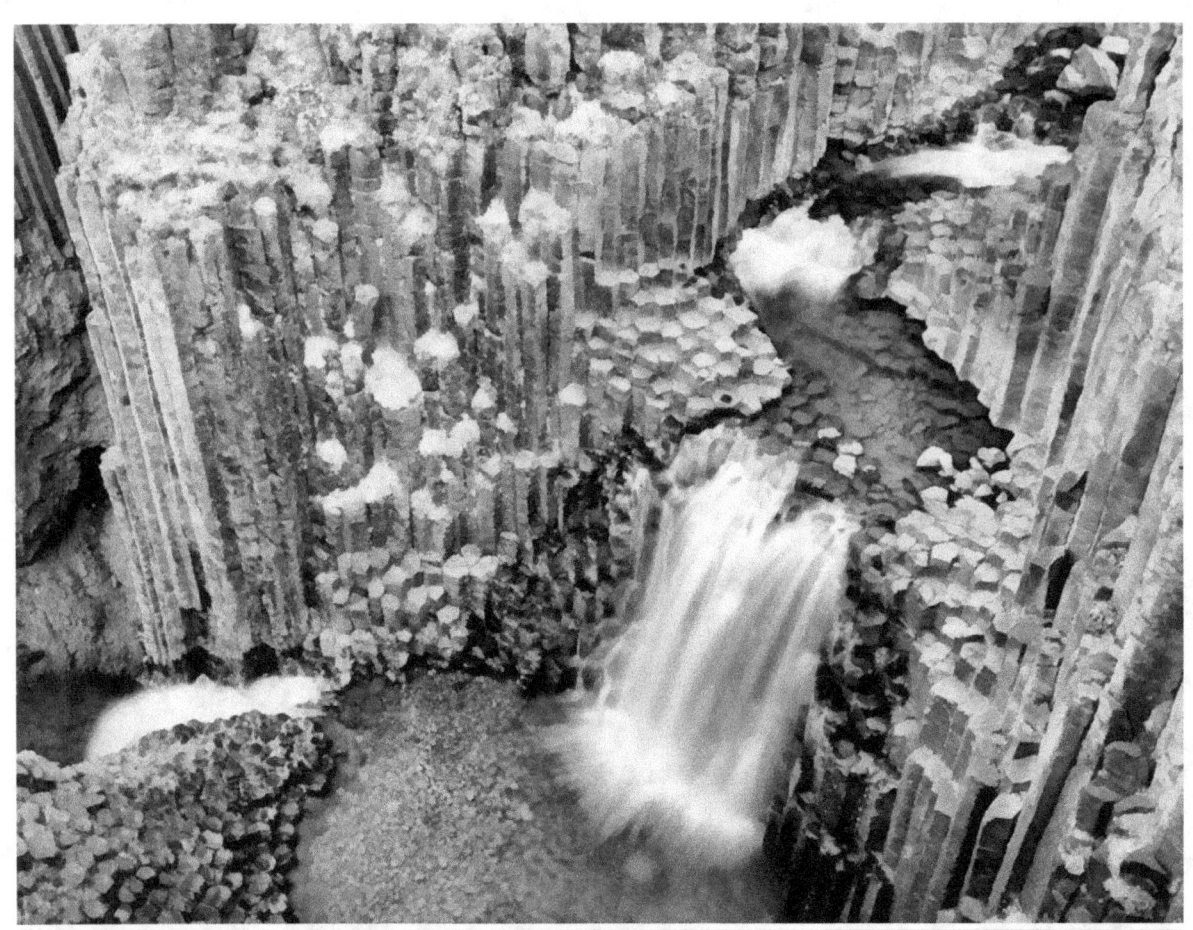

Joan Miro (Spain). Reproduction of Original by him, using Palette Knife.

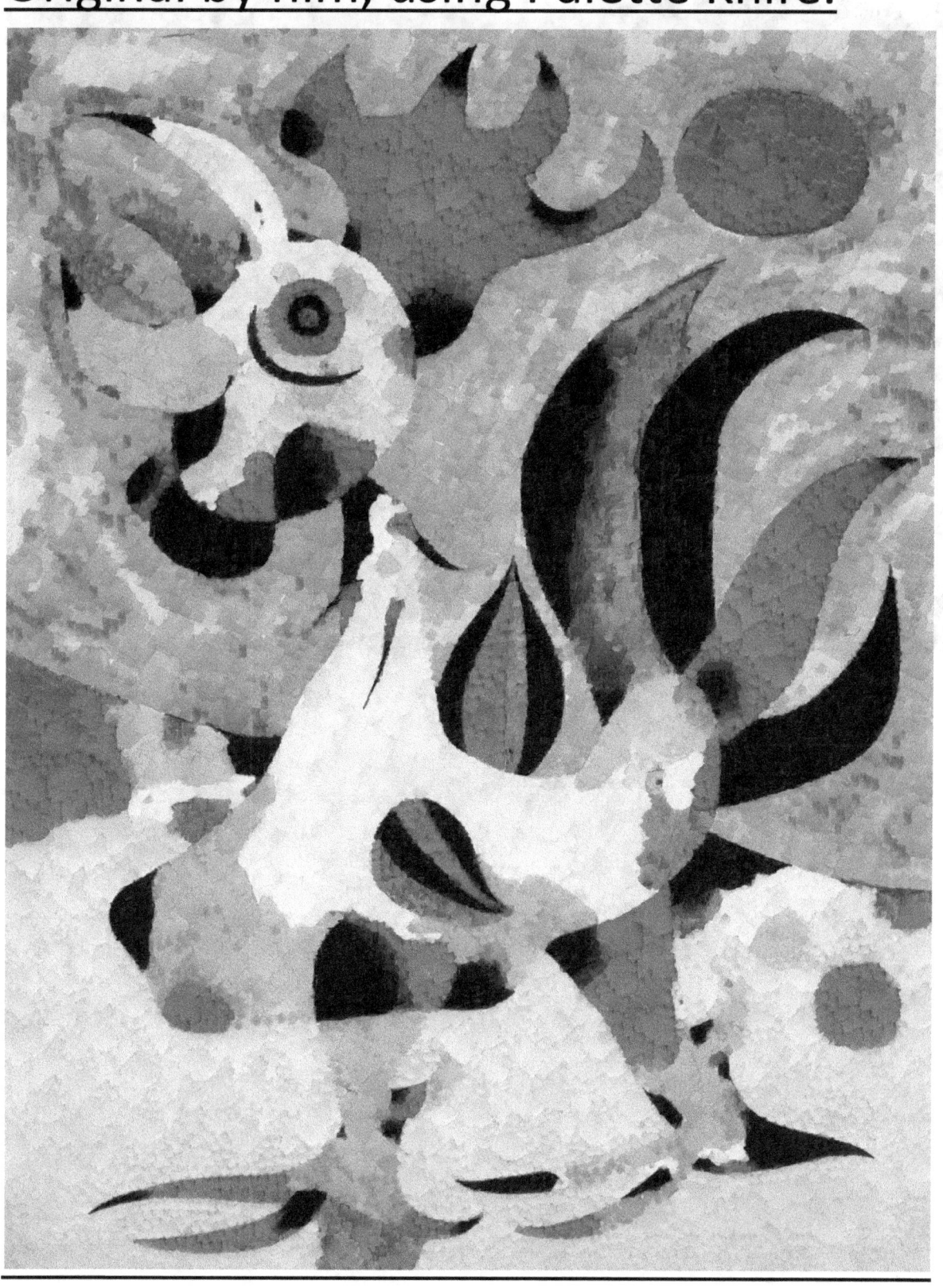

Cezanne inspired art:

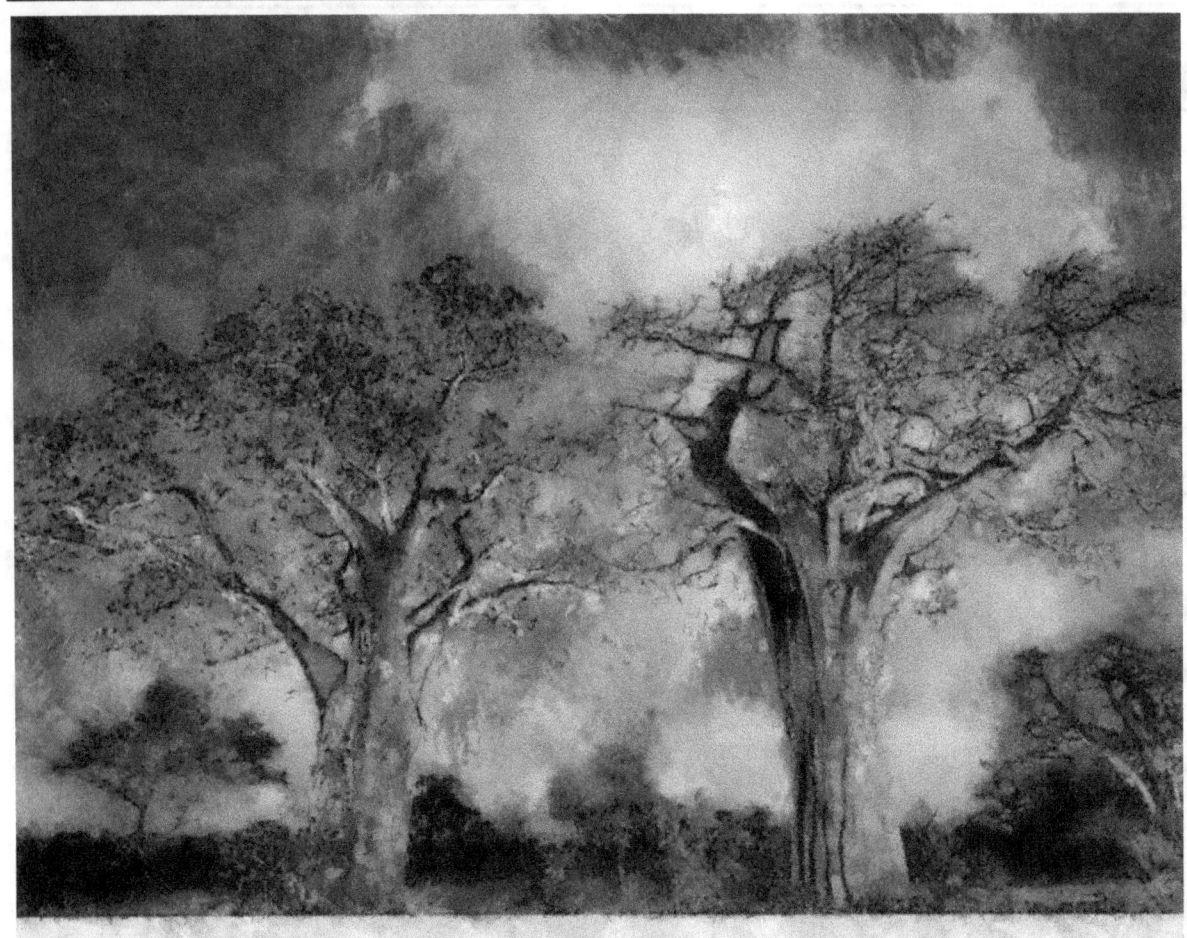

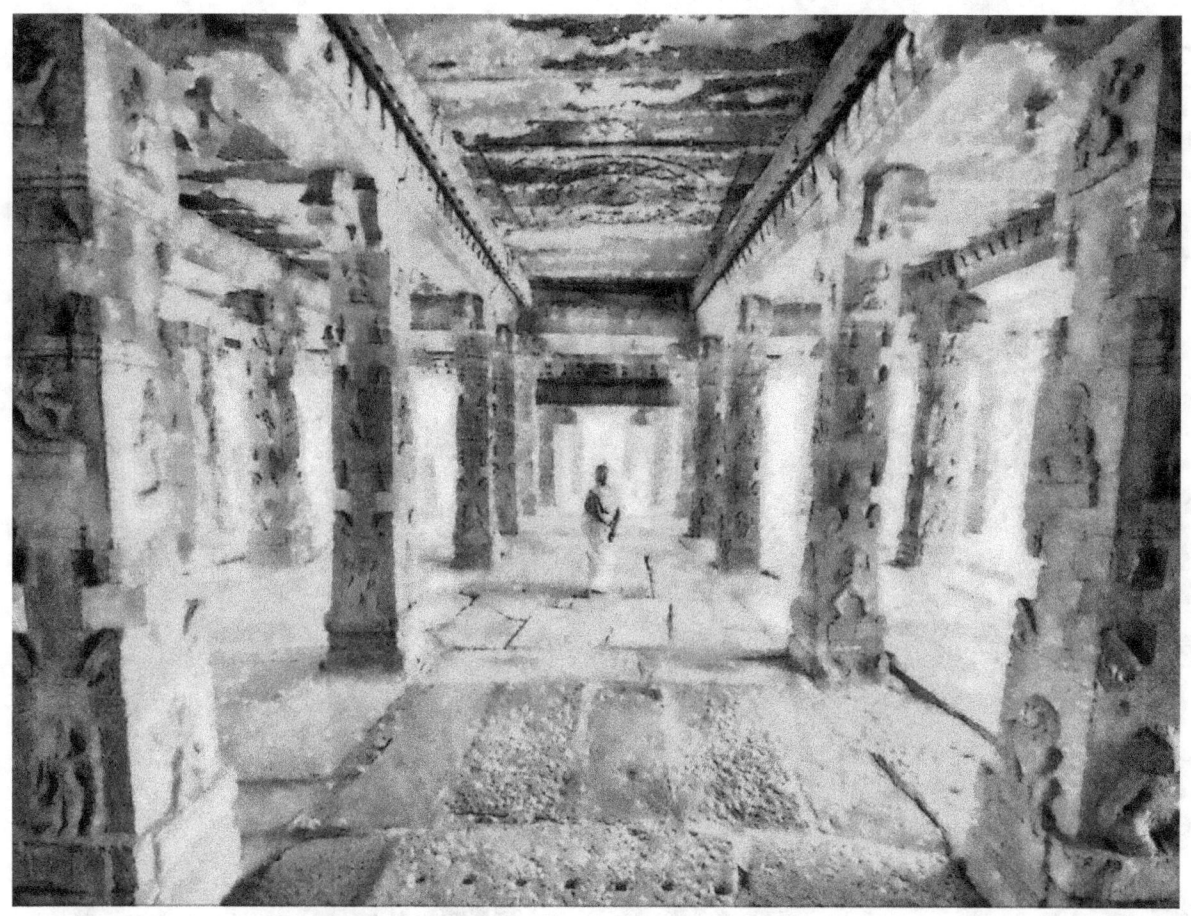

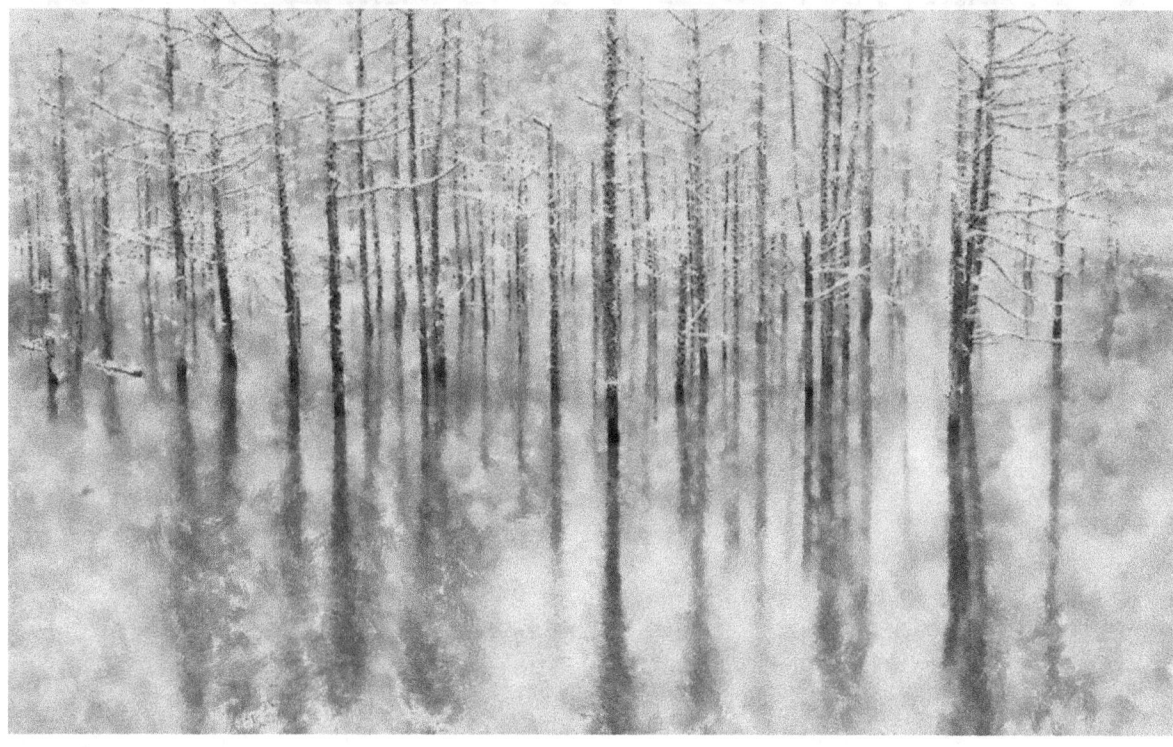

Joaquin Sorolla (Spain):

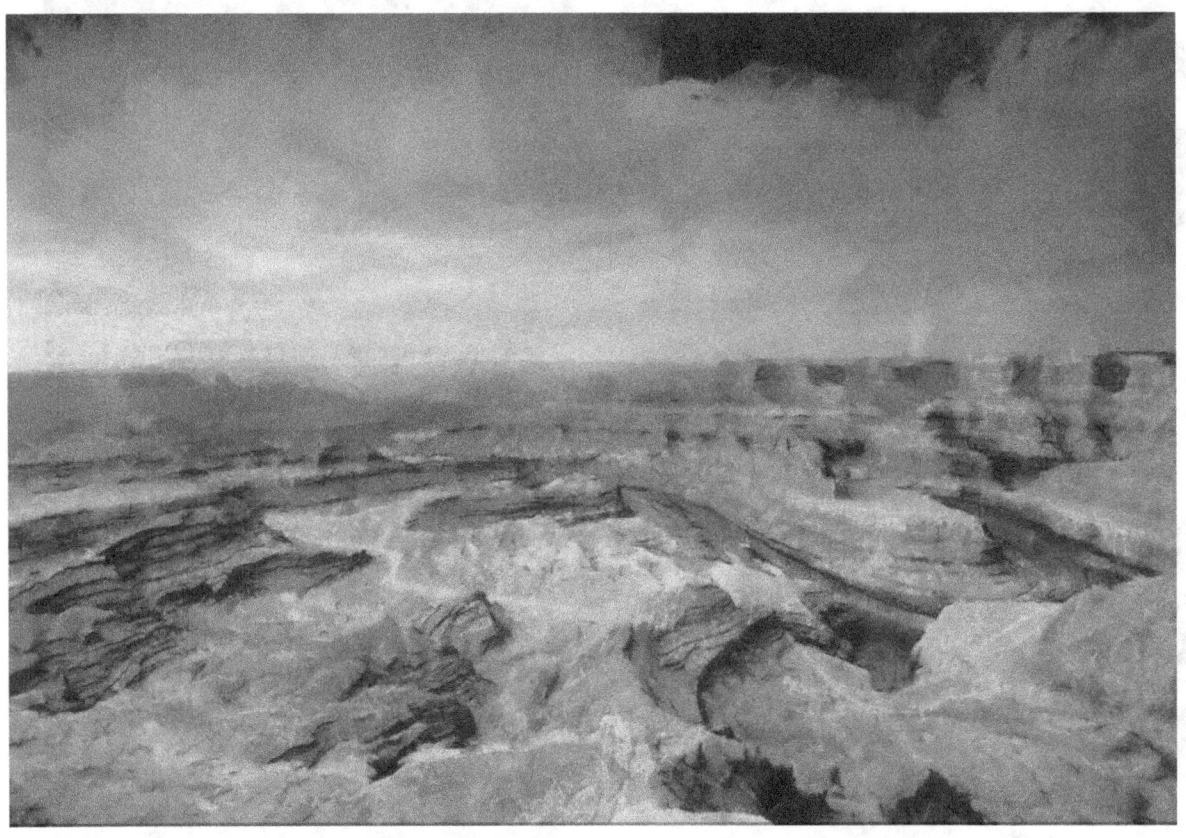

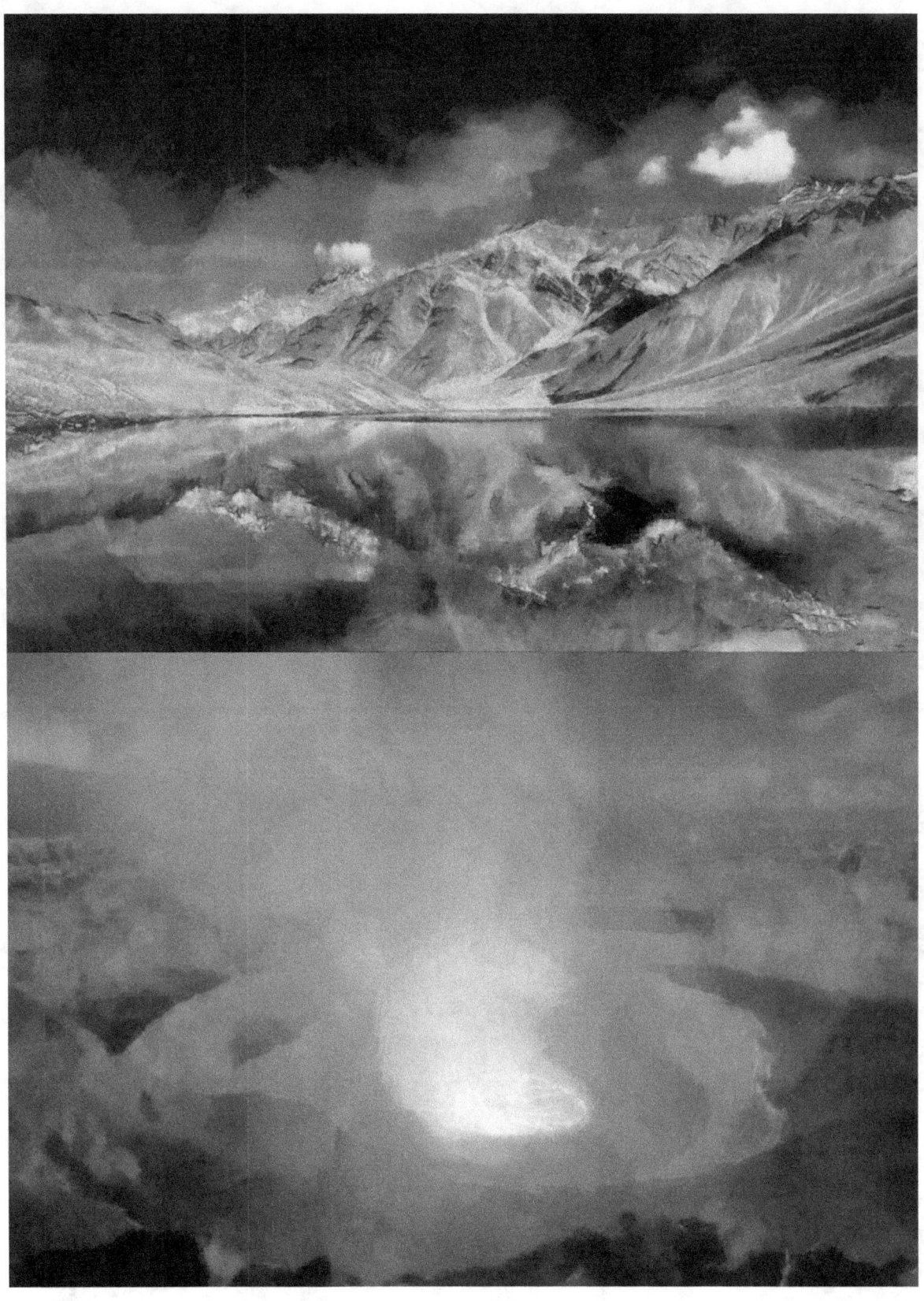

Cezanne:

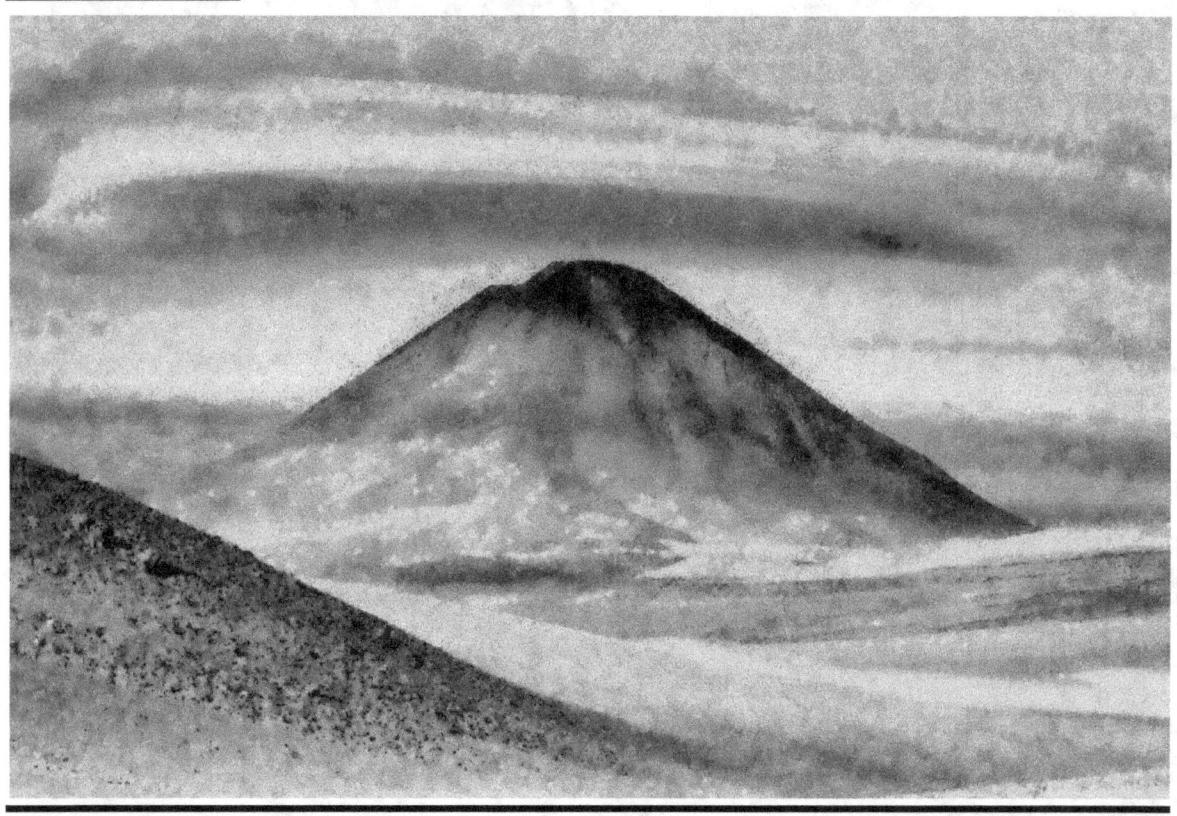

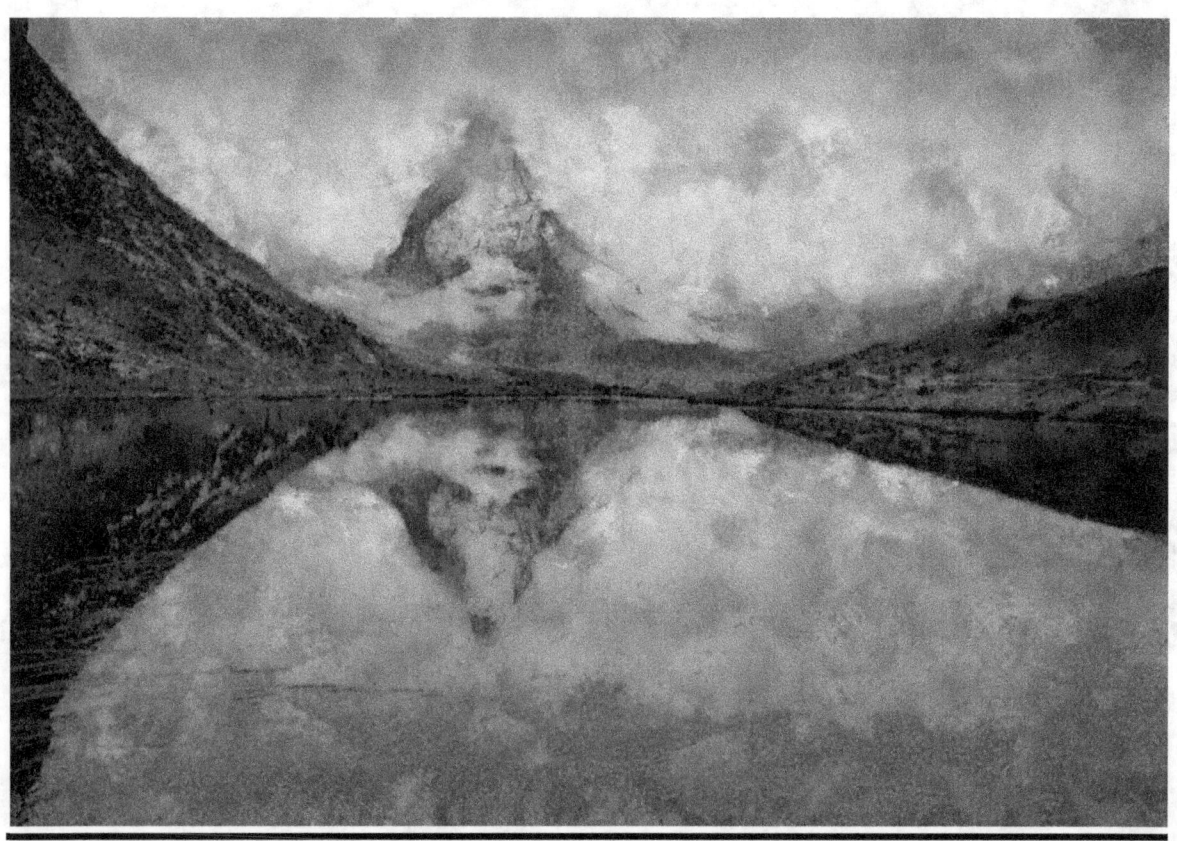

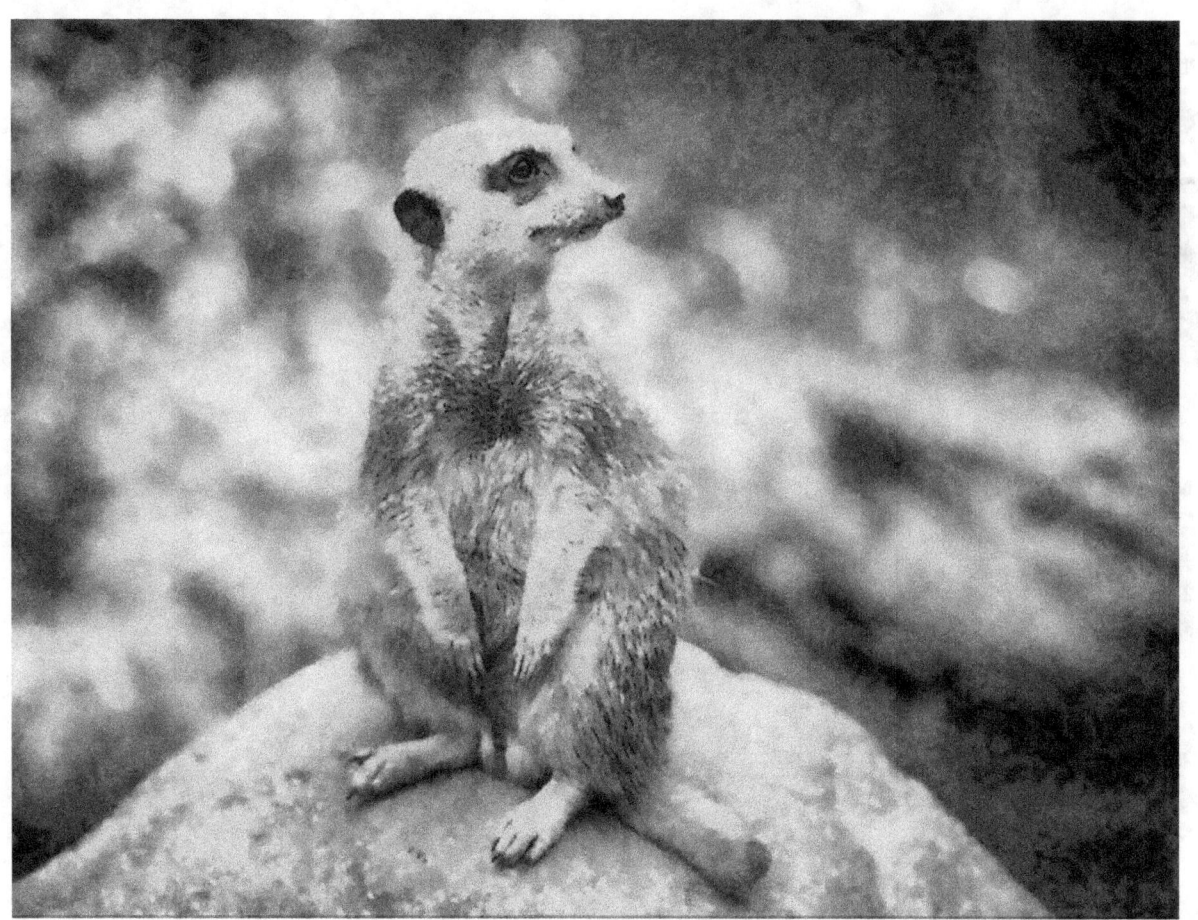

Gustav Klimt (Austria) inspired: 'Music' Painting.

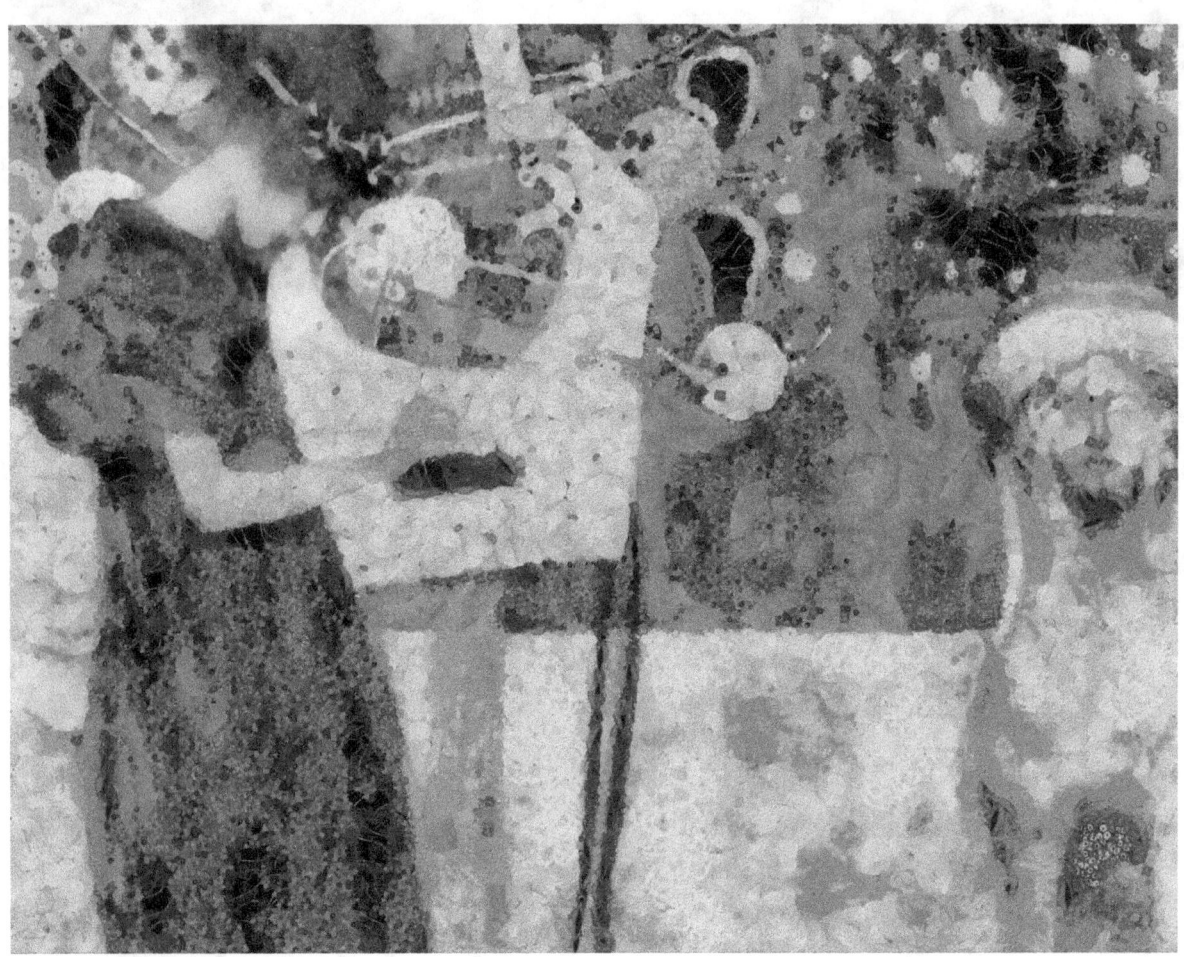

Joaquin Sorolla (Spain):

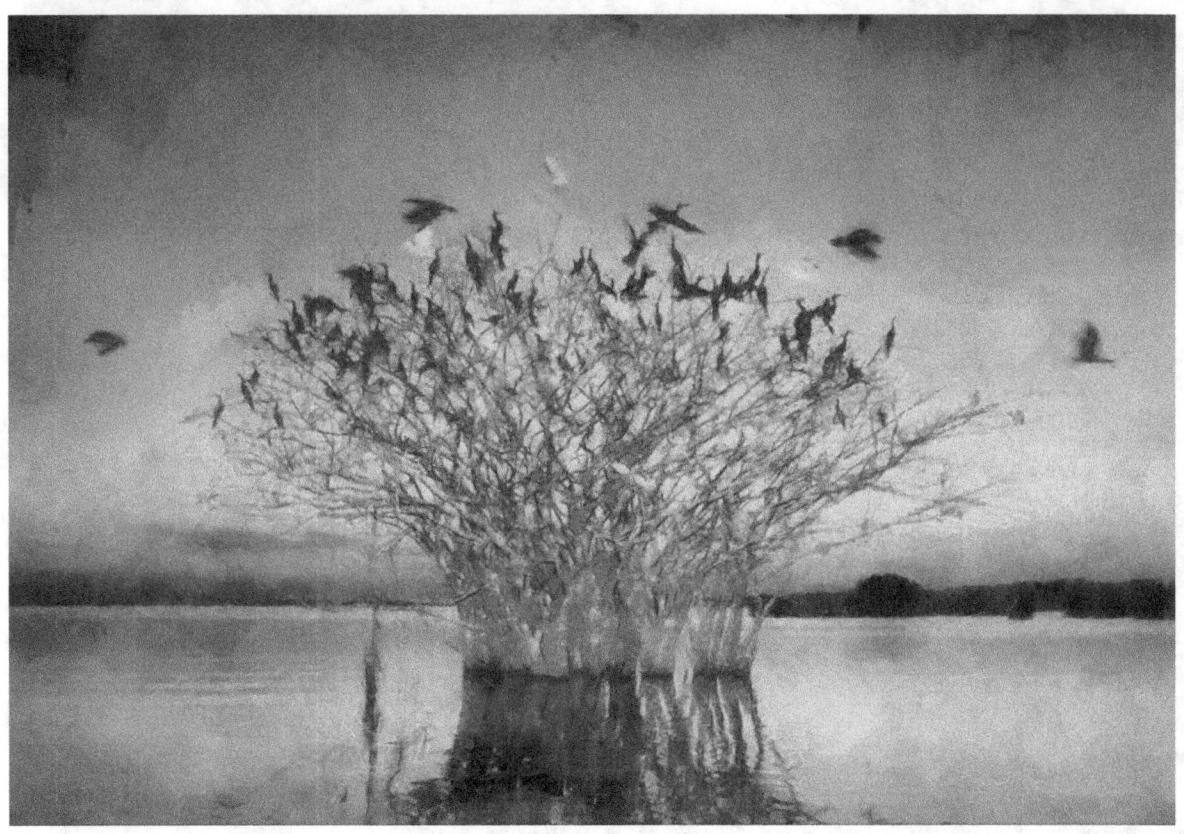

Claude Monet (France):

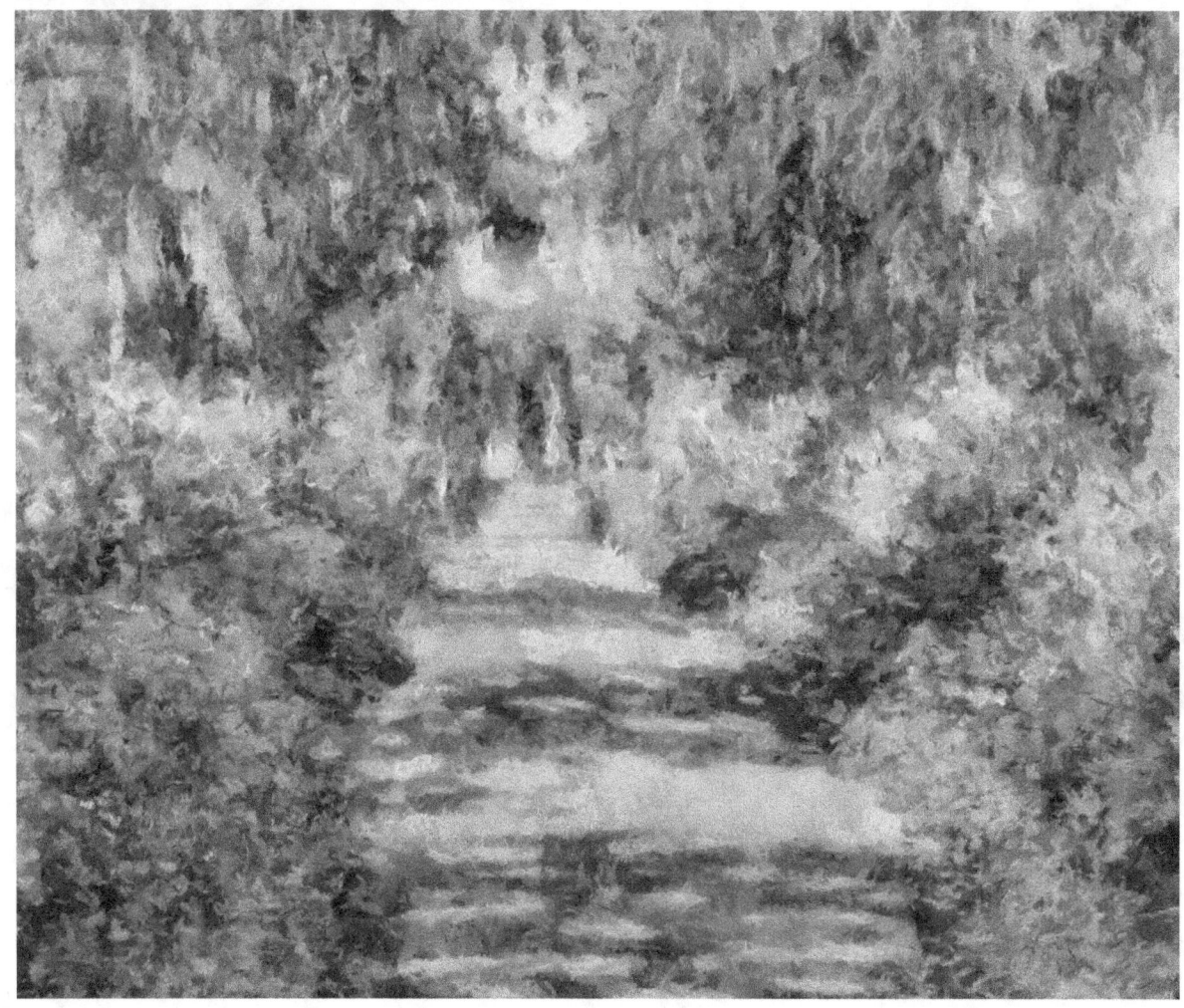

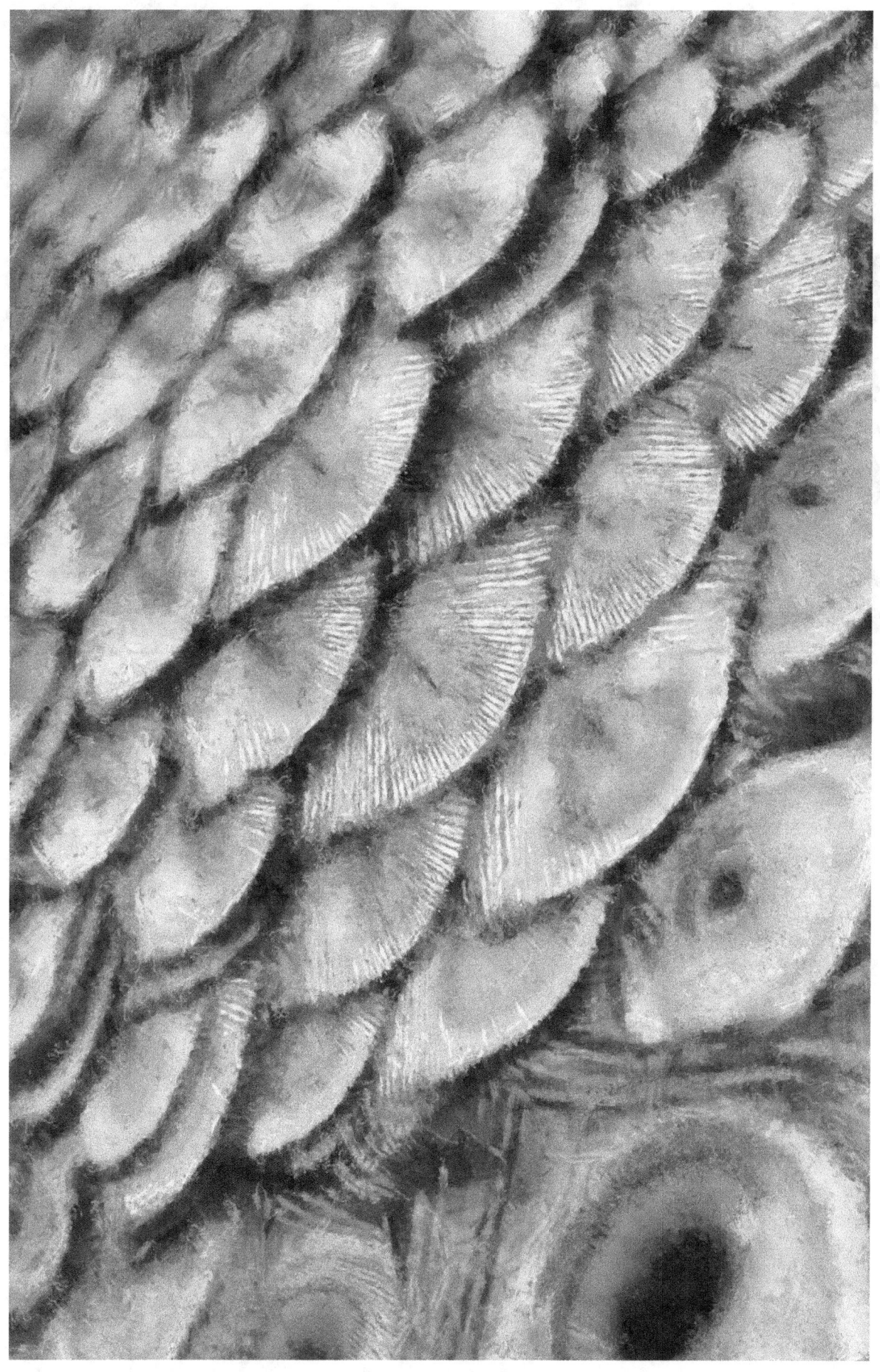

Cezanne:

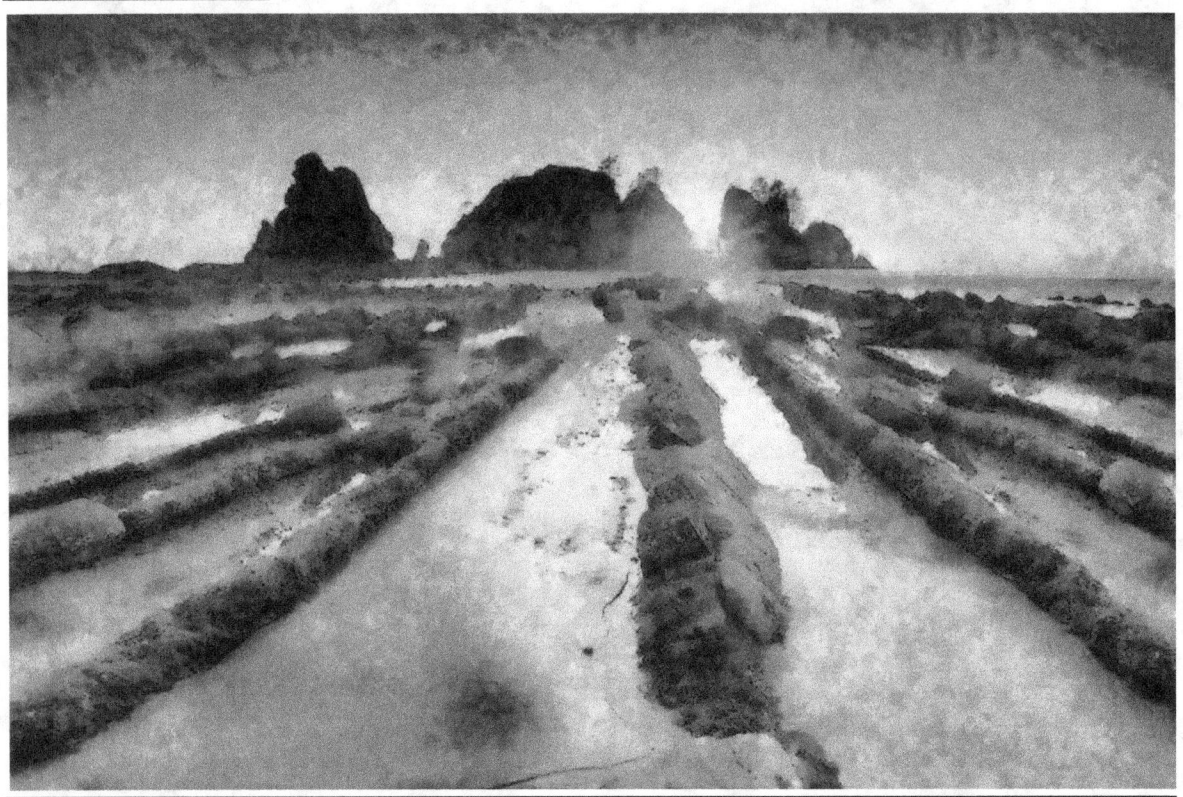

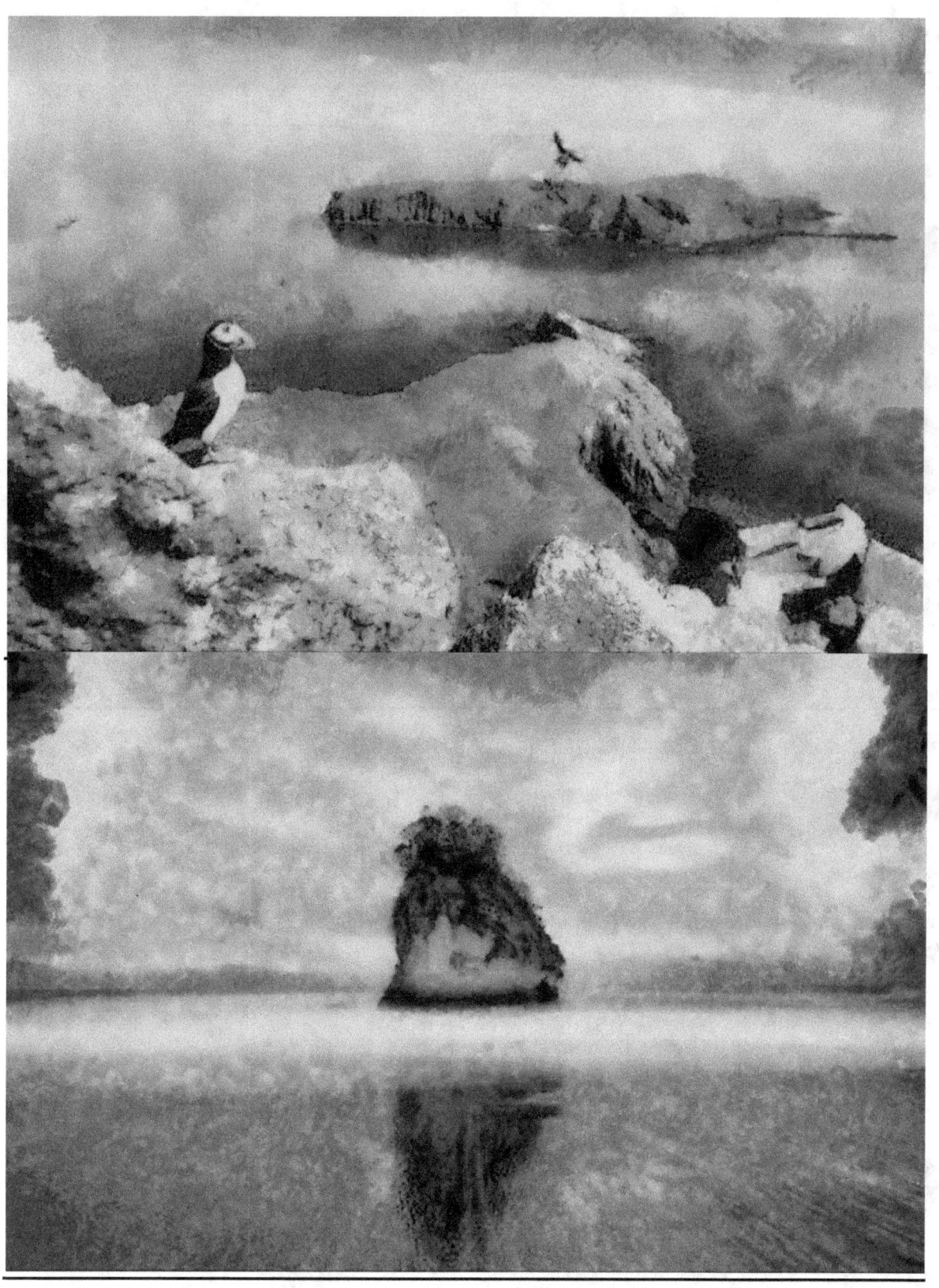

Photo-Realism:

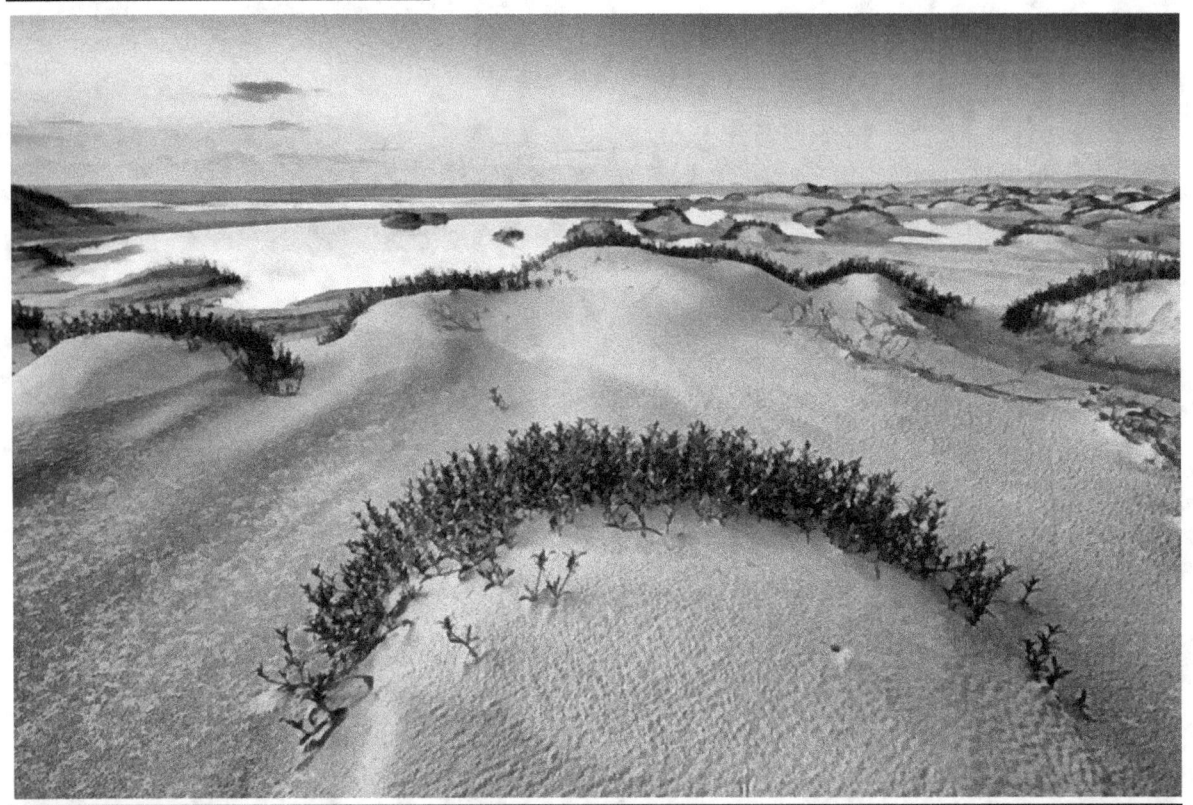

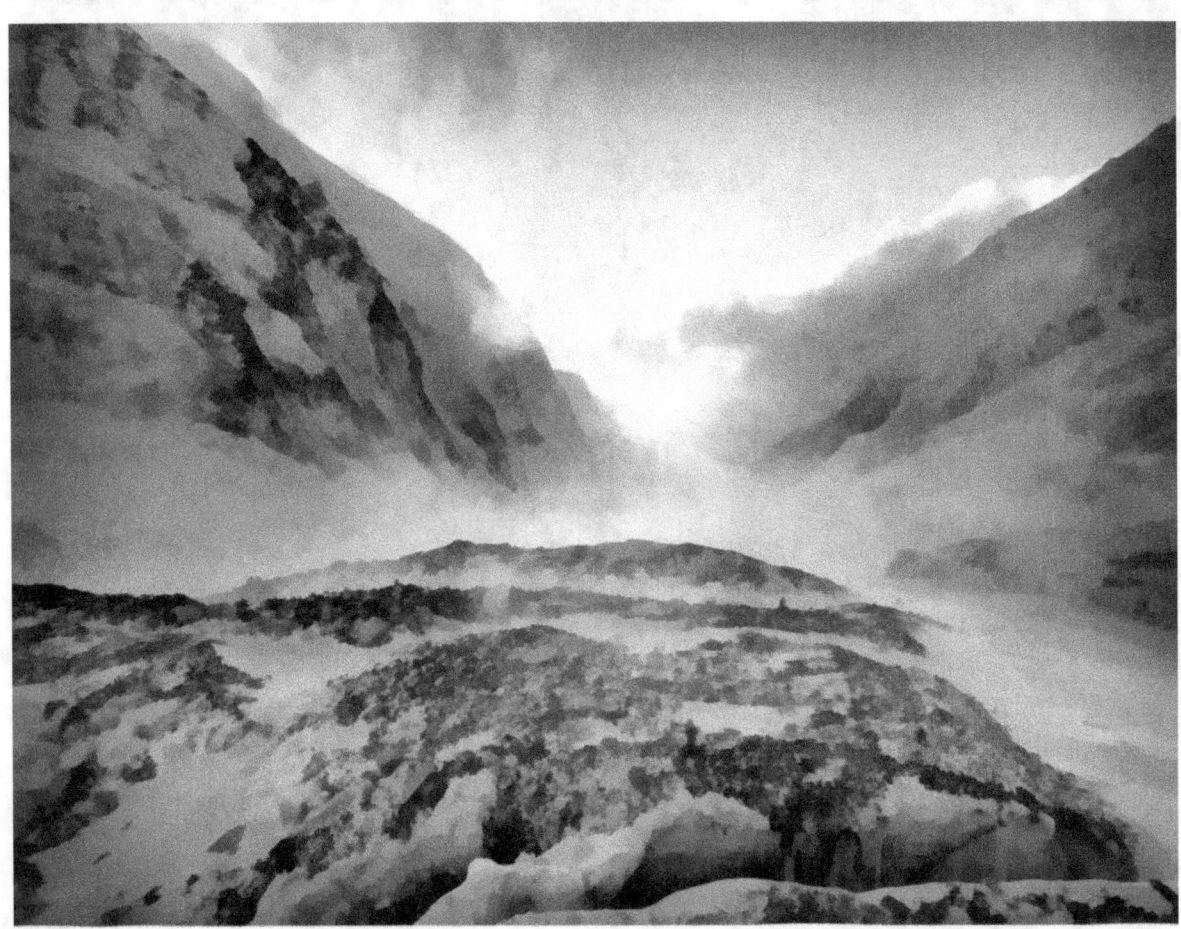

Cezanne (France):

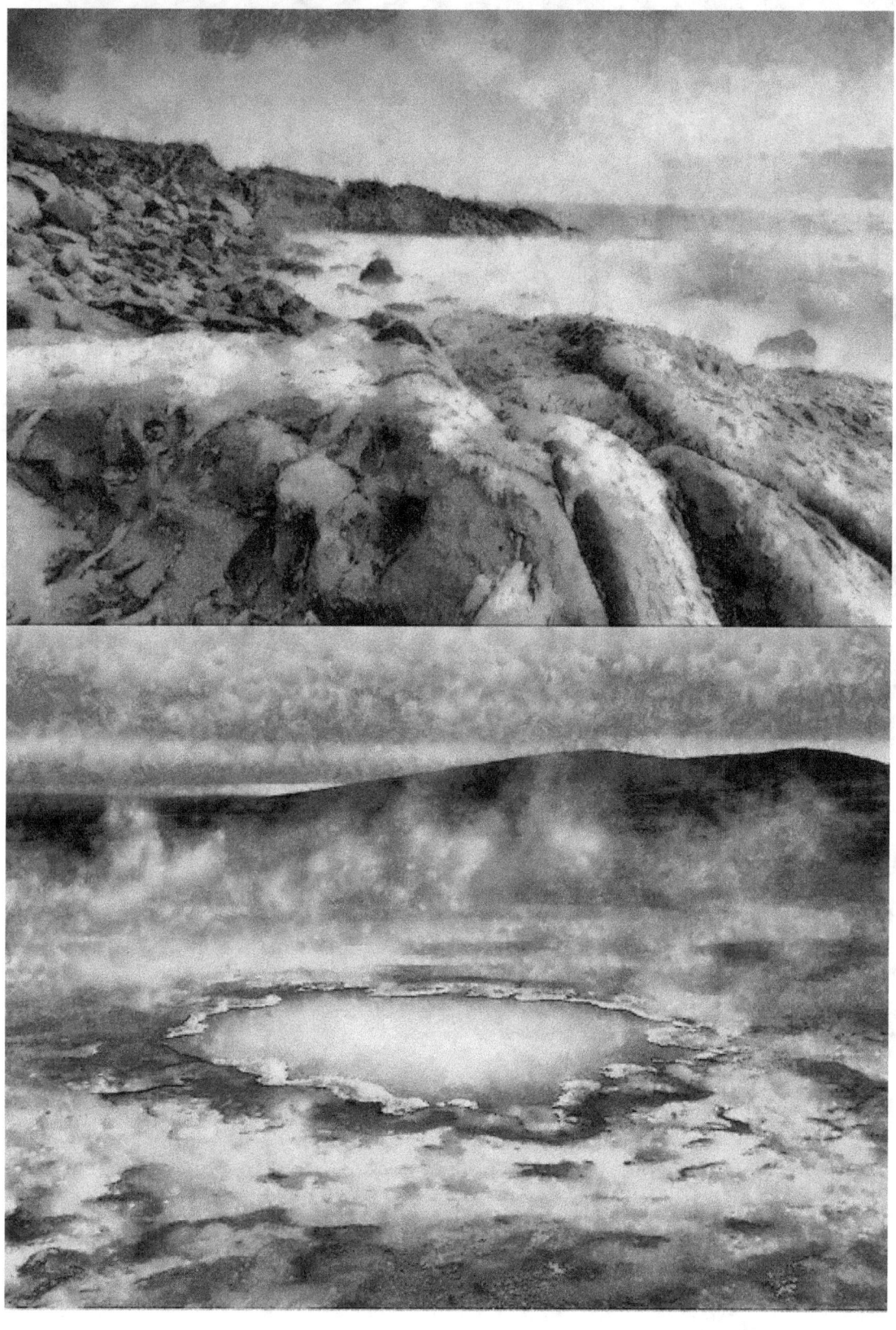

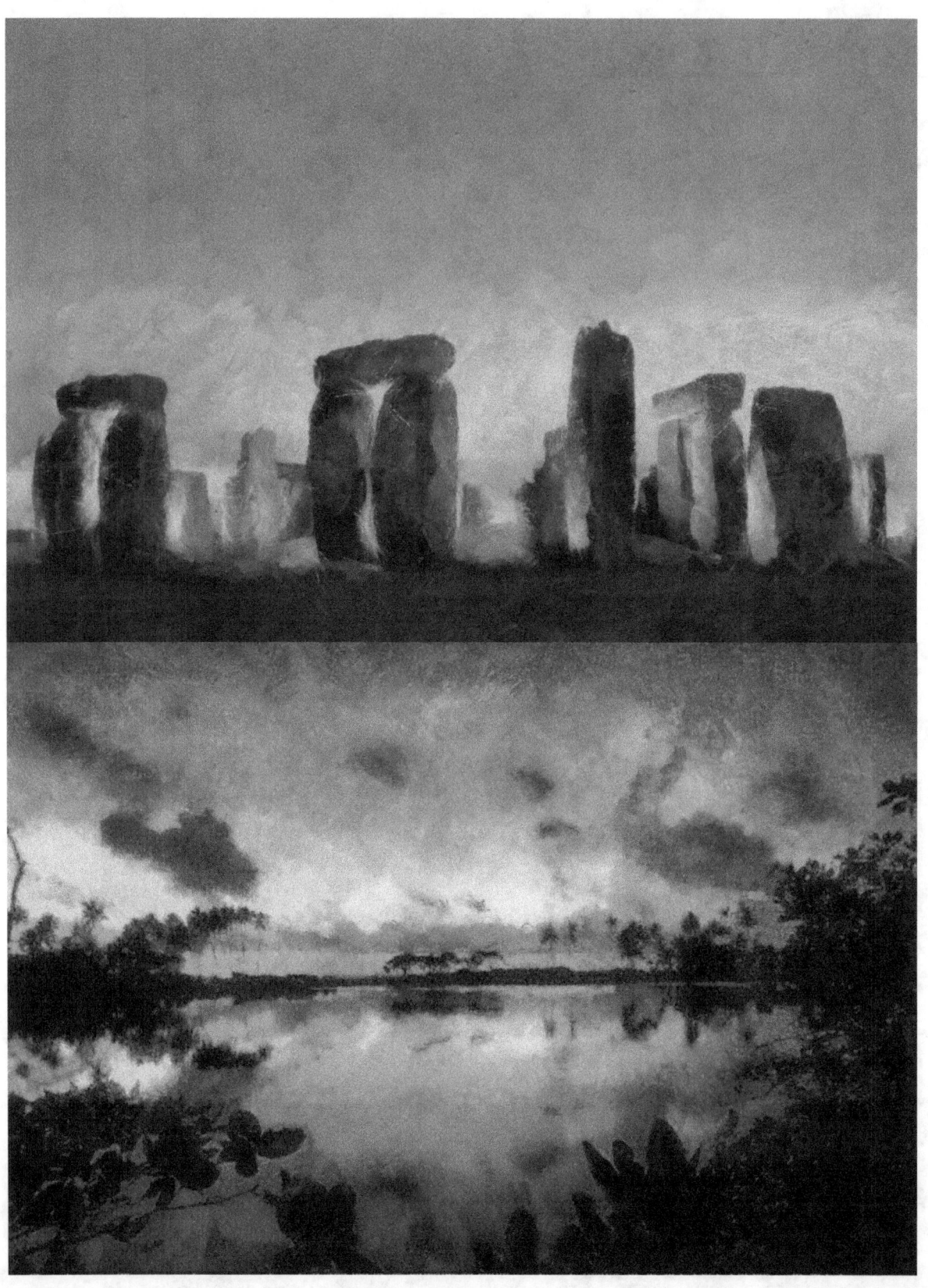

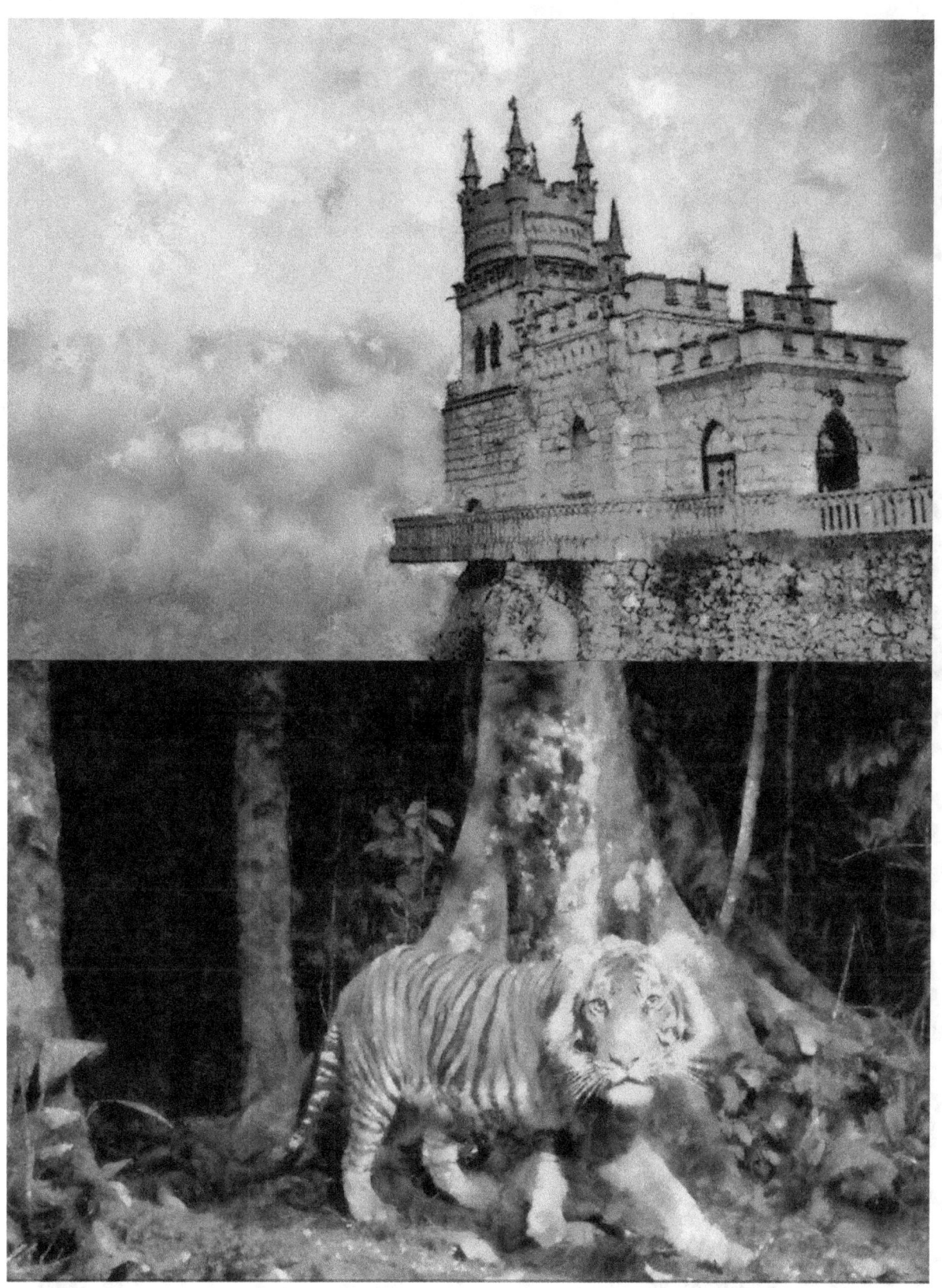

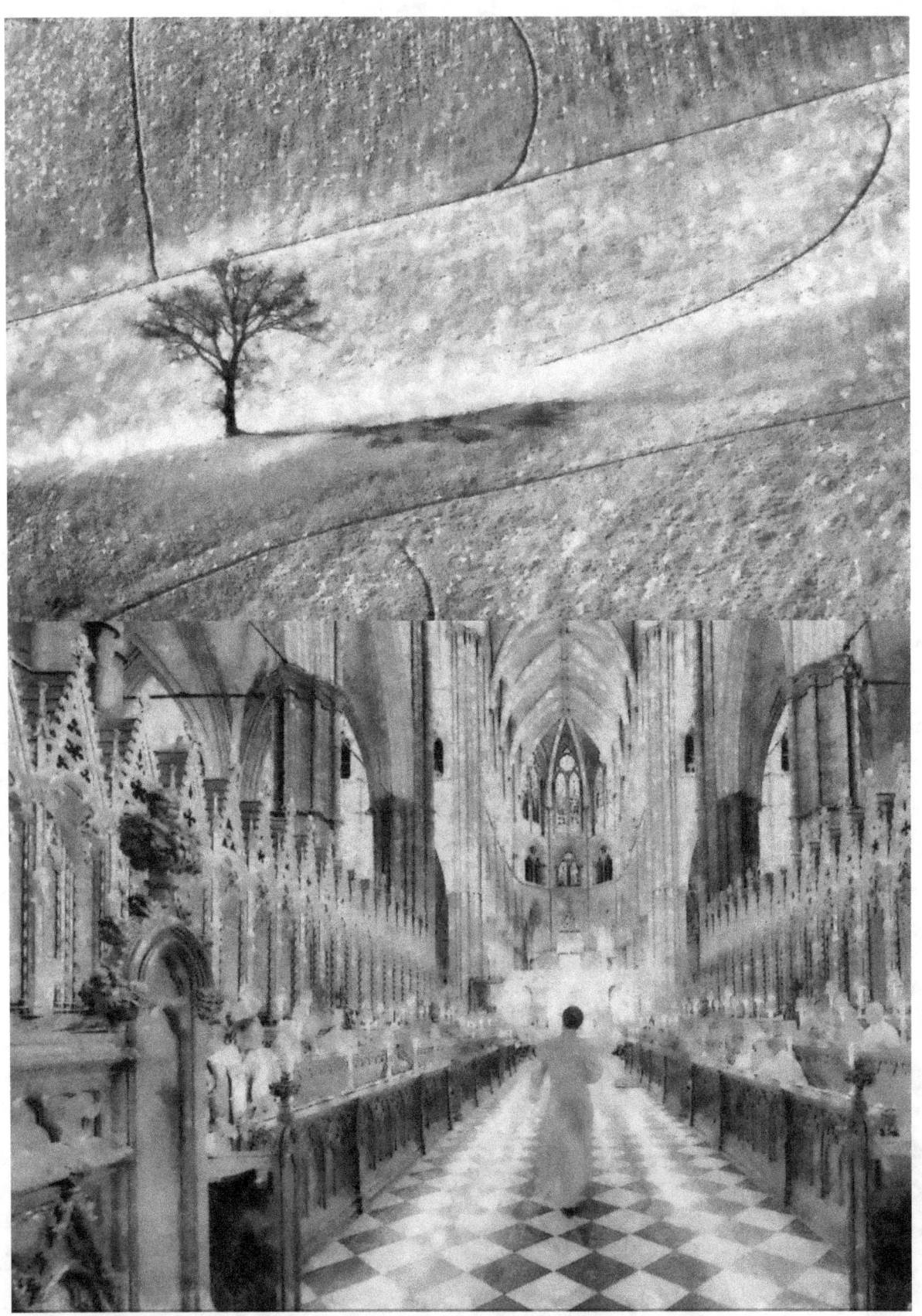

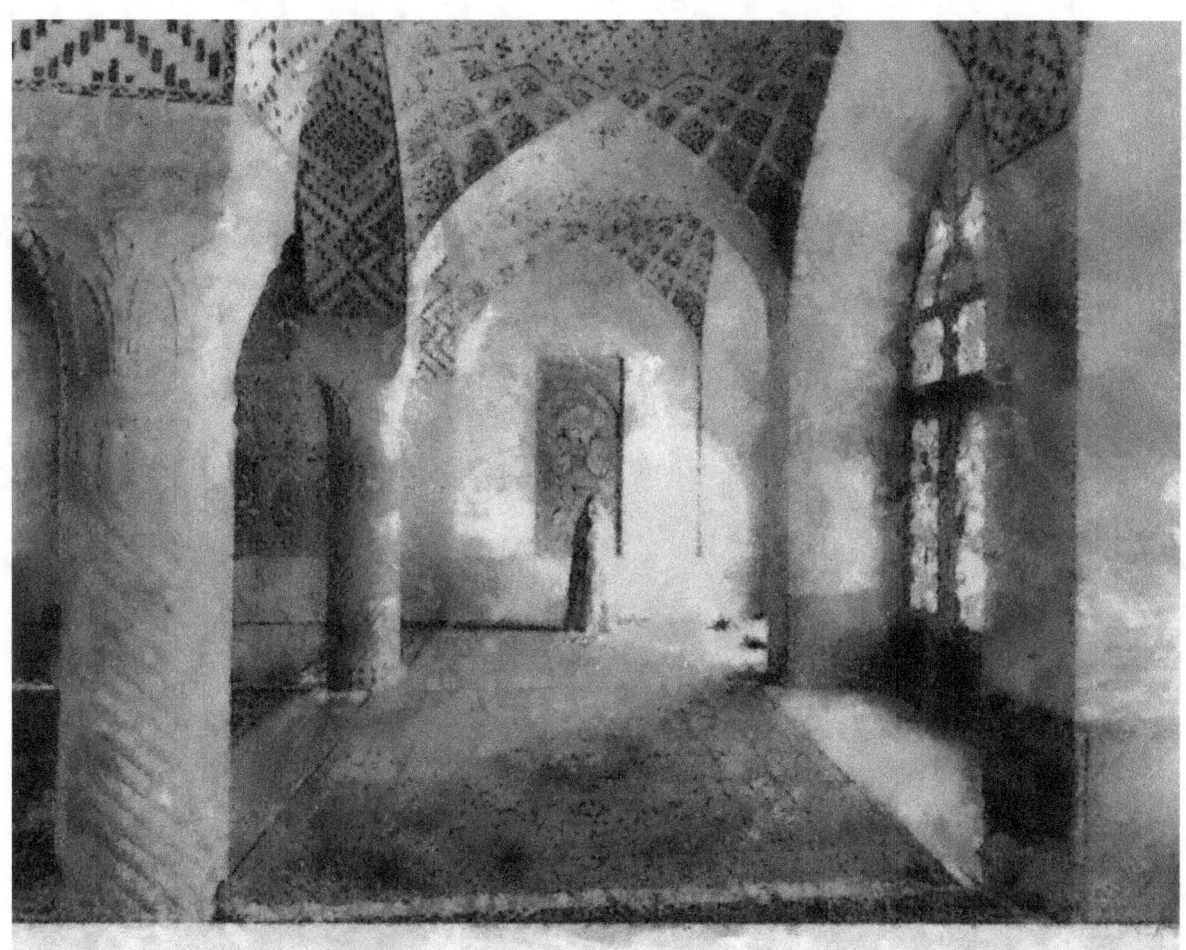

Edvard Munch (Norway): (Pastel Version)

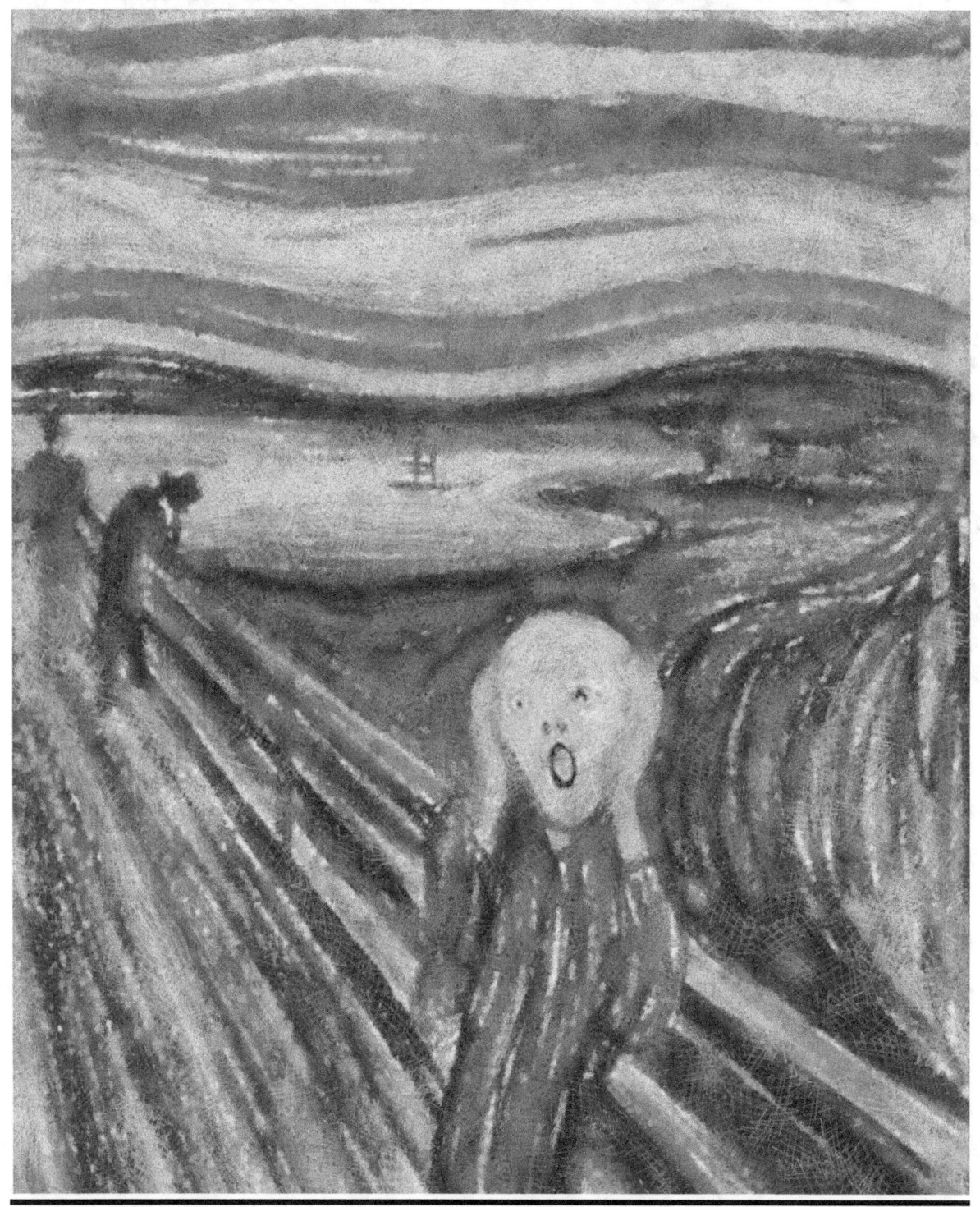

Joaquin Sorolla (Spain):

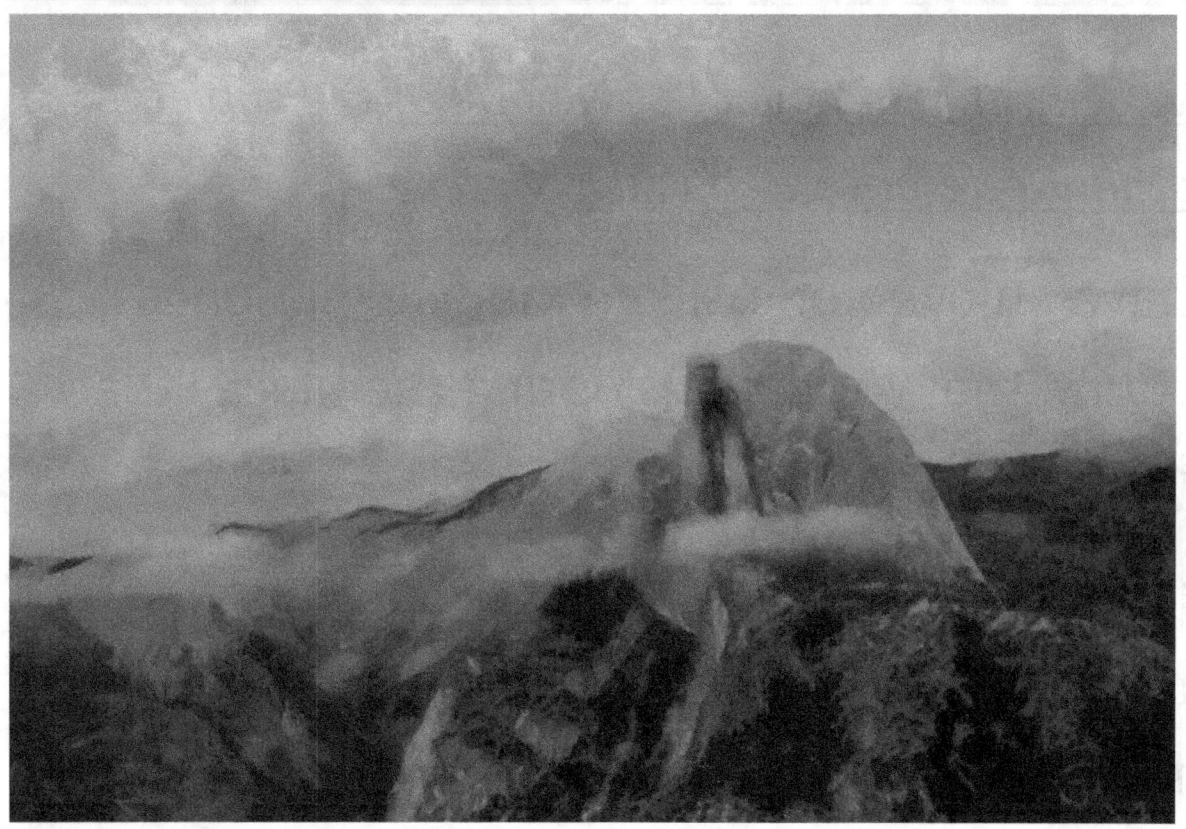

Van Gogh (Dutch):

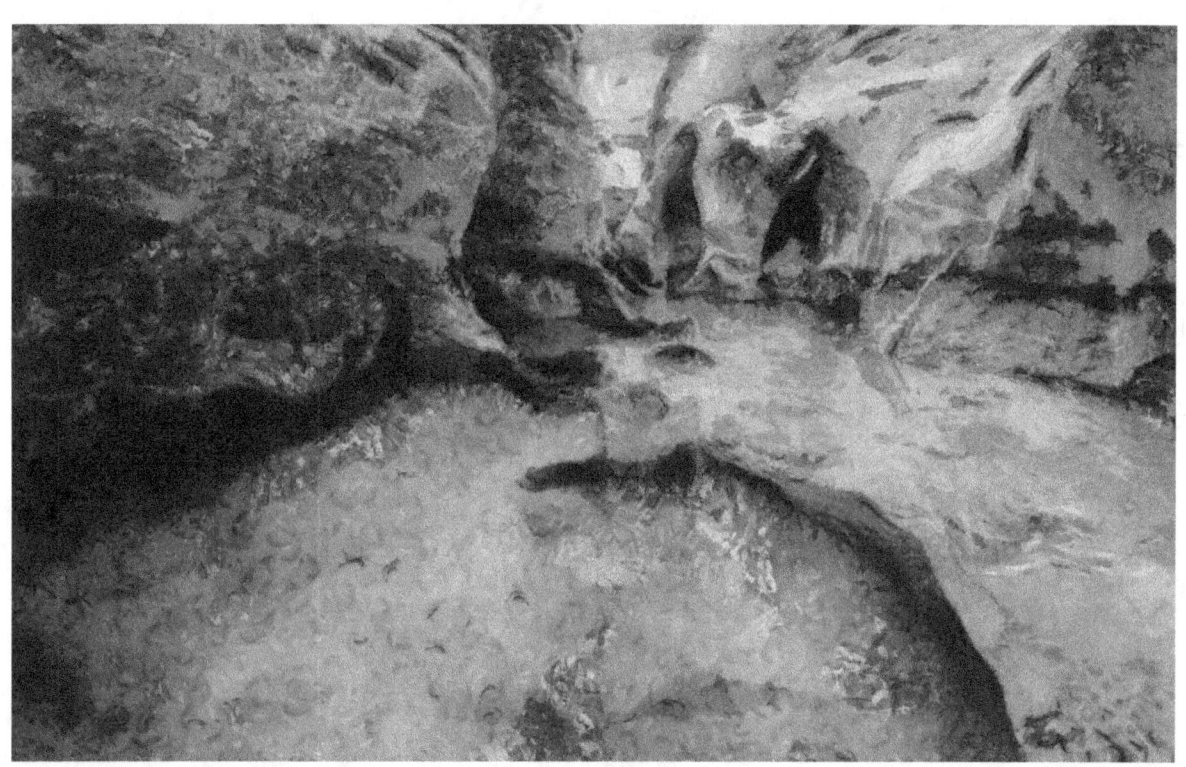

Art Theory & Culture around the World.

(*Myself rambling over knowledge of the subject without reference to books*).

I have enjoyed or disliked many experiences around the world, considering the places that I have travelled.

I having travelled to France ie. South of France & also Barcelona, Spain, have seen lots of Pablo Picasso art paintings, as the Spanish artist was a resident those days there in Spain.

To my knowledge, Picasso born in 1881, was as a child extremely gifted and prodigious in art. He studied in art school a few years ahead of his class. His father was also an Spanish artist by profession. So he came from a background of painters.

Famous Spanish artists I feel tend to project

the graphic scenes of suffering, hardship and at the same time preserving personality, that is to say personal touches, and humanity without becoming too impersonal. Most of the hardships represent war, like WWII.

Salvador Dali,another Spanish artist, was a person depicting surreal art. To reach out to the subconscious, almost unreal pictures, that perhaps relive nightmarish or scary, perturbing or disturbing scenarios. His artwork I feel is most imaginative, as it does not depict realistic art.

Joan Miro, is a Spanish Abstract Artist, that paints weird, strange pictorial painting, that at times do not seem humanistic, and very much out of this world.

Interestingly the Spanish Artist, Miro died in 1983, on Christmas Day (25th Dec 1983).

Talking about a great Austrian Artist, namely, Gustav Klimt: He was an Austrian Symbolistic Painter. What I make of 'symbolistic' painters was they used several similar patterns to create an overall effect.

Gustav Klimt used to paint with the overuse of Gold in his paintwork. An example of gold in his paintwork is his 'Portrait of Adele-Bloch', which was and still is at present one of the most expensive paintings in the world.

Kasimir Malevich, a Russian Geometric Abstract Artist, born in 1879, was a pioneer of Abstract Art with Geometric with squares, triangles. USSR was formed in 1922, and he died shortly in the 1930's. Aside from art, USSR predominantly developed with military interests.

Geometry Abstract Art represented impersonal and structural interests, rather than people.

Amedeo Modigliani was an Italian portrait painter who was a competitor of Picasso in the late 19th and early 20th century.

He used elongated portrait pictures of women and men to create a interesting effect. Essentially preserving personal characteristics at the same time introducing something innovative, those were the ideas of Picasso and Modigliani.

It was a unique idea of his, which made his paintings characteristic and authentically original by these artists.

Van Gogh was defined as a Post-Impressionist painter, as he used beautiful sprightly, vivid colors in his artwork, which was too bold and outrageous than to defined as Impressionism.

(*I have written a definition of Impressionism on my website: www.simhadrisoftware.com*

I myself was not familiar with this term, when I started out digital painting, so excuse myself. Thank you all).

Van Gogh used a special brushstroke style,

which was really an unique signature of his work. His work the Sunflowers (1888), now housed in the National Gallery in London, UK, I have had the privilege of seeing when a medical student in London in 1999.

Swirling and curving brushstrokes of Van Gogh, which make his paintings easy to recognise by the passer-by or first-time observer. An example of this phenomenon is shown in 'Starry Night', a famous painting by Van Gogh.

Claude Monet (France), was a very successful French painter, that painted most beautiful gardens in Giverny, France. The paintwork of lovely flowers, and trees is most aesthetically pleasing to observe.

Claude Monet, was very successful artist and became a millionaire in his days. Claude Monet I believe was an Impressionist painter.

He introduced Impressionism, a special style of painting to the world. That is what makes Claude Monet, very remarkable to the art world.

Pierre-Auguste Renoir, is another French painter of the 19th Century. He painted mainly paintings of personal scenes, people rather than scenery and impersonal objects.

He used paintwork, that scintillated with light, reflected light, at least that is what I believe.

Frank Weston Benson, was an US artist, of the 19th Century, who painted the murals of the Library of Congress, in Washington DC,USA, which is one of the largest and most beautiful Libraries in the world. I have been inside the Library of Congress,in 1998, and I believe it was ever so beautiful to observe as an architectural building.

Benson's artwork is easily observed by fuzzy, blurred sunny scenes, almost like the Mediterranean seaside.

Mark Rothko was a modern US painter, based in New York. He painted simplistic rectangles of color, and was known as an Abstract Expressionist artist as he with simplisticity reflected shapes and rectangles of color with 'expression'.

John Singer Sargent, is another US 19th Century painter who travelled including England. His paintwork also is characteristic. Essentially, one must observe my websites to appreciate and distinguish his unique painting style.

That I feel is the correct way and method to notice different artists characteristic painting.

Francis Bacon,was a most illustrated UK artist, who at present (2014) has the most expensive artwork in an auction.

What I make of his artwork, is that he show weird, dark and strange scenes perhaps reminiscent of unreal, disturbed scenes. To decipher the paintings significance and purpose is difficult.

Edvard Munch (Norway), is a painter who painted, creepy, frightening, horrific and sometime scary scenes. He painted with dark, and dreary colors.

Paul Cezanne (France), would have a colorful, sprightly, palette. Shades of bright color blending with one another.

I must say, that if someone was to present to me a Cezanne, from another artist, I would be able to distinguish.

Cezanne had a characteristic way of painting, that is very easy to notice. The **most expensive** painting at present is the 'Card Players' by Cezanne (approx. $250 million dollars) sold at an auction, as of March 2014.

Paul Gauguin was also a French painter, and a painter of the 'synthetism' movement.

I have painted some still life to his style, which is shown on his websites.

I am not totally familiar with this, and whole art theory of this would require a lot of research and study.

John Constable, and English Romantic Painter of the 18th Century, painted lovely green and earthly-colored palette of countryside scenery. I have digitally painted some paintings like this.

Artwork through the Ages

As we travel through the ages, I feel that art paintings has become more detached, impersonal, and whilst previously artwork depicted people, animals and social scenes, Modern Art reflects impersonal bias. I feel perhaps this is due the world becoming more materialistic perhaps, for instance there has been with time greater inventions, and discoveries whilst the world has developed.

To explain warfare, has increased conflict and

does not really beautify or improve the image of the planet. That is frankly, what I believe.

Though in order to compete, compromise and negotiate, I concede wars must be necessary, that is what I feel.

Travelling around the World.

I have travelled the world, and in a lot of places I must admit I really did not have a good experience, however having said that I found visiting places, observing beautiful buildings and meeting people, and family friends very interesting.

For instance, Eiffel Tower, I observed in Paris in the mid 1980's as a kid. 'Sacre-Coeur' was also a lovely white religious monument there in France.

Whilst visiting Edinburgh,UK, I also observed Edinburgh Castle,perched next to a cliff.

Later I decided to digitally paint all of them.

Thanking you,

Vijay Simhadri

(Artist of Digital Paintings on the Internet)

www.ingramcontent.com/pod-product-compliance
Lightning Source LLC
Chambersburg PA
CBHW081614200526
45167CB00020B/4025